ONE-ROOM
COUNTRY SCHOOL

❖

ONE-ROOM
COUNTRY SCHOOL

South Dakota Stories

Edited by
Norma C. Wilson and Charles L. Woodard

South Dakota Humanities Foundation
Brookings, South Dakota

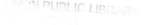

Library of Congress Cataloging in Publication Data

Wilson, Norma C. and Woodard, Charles L.
One-Room Country School: South Dakota Stories

Norma C. Wilson and Charles L. Woodard
1. Schools — South Dakota — History
2. Education — Midwest — Memoirs
ISBN 0-9632157-5-2

Third Edition June 2001
2000 copies printed
Manufactured in the United States of America
by Quality Quick Print, Inc.
Composition by Media One, Inc., Sioux Falls, SD

ACKNOWLEDGMENTS

With appreciation for your contributions, we thank all who wrote or submitted memoirs and who assisted us in our research and writing: Leonora Abrahamson, Janet Andersen, Crystal Ashley, Mary Valentine Bedsaul, Fred A. Beeman, Harold Benson, Shirley Benz, Faye Bertram, Herbert W. Blakely, Joyce Boegler, Carol Boies, Rozella Bracewell, Marvin Braun, Phylis Brunken, Donald E. Buss, The Chilson Collection (I.D. Weeks Library, University of South Dakota), Conde Centennial Committee, Lavonne L. Crook, Lorraine Crouch, Dick Deboer, Phyllis Dixon, Sandra A. Dyson, Sharon Eggers, Isabelle Hedman Elliott, Mary Gederos, Ruth Graves Ellis, Winifred Bertrand Fawcett, John Fiksdal,

Ada May Geppert Foster, Ruth I. Culver Foster, Leo E. Giacometto, Mary Giesler, Alden Gillings, Harold Gunn, Irene Hansen, Michael Haug, Betty Rupkalvis Herron, Ellen Reisdorph Hieb, Rolf N. Hovey, Jon Huber, Clara M. Hoffer, Adam Hoffer, Barbara Hundstad, Art Huseboe, Doris Eggers Huseboe, Eileen Iverson, Dennis Johnson, Duane E. Johnson, Bertha O. Johnson, Gertrude Johnson, Mary Dougherty Johnson, Shirley E. Juracek, William A. Justice, Myra Kalb, Bertha Kessel, Jeannette Kinyon, Pauline Kjergaard, Wayne Knutson, Helen Medeck Kremer, Lily Kruse, Magdalena Schmidt Kyte, Betty Larrington, Carl Lindblad, Verla Lindblad, Nancy Losacker, Ardelle A. Lundeen, Eva Madden, Jeanne Jones Manzer, Gerald Matson, Leona Anderson McInerny, Media One, Leonard C. Meyer, Eleanore Rowan Moe, Norma Moller, James A. Nachtigal, Ollie Napesni, Leo Neifer, Kathy Snyder Nelson, Emma Sittner Nelson, Patricia Sougstad-Nelson, Shawn Oligmueller, Marilyn Owen, Melanie L. Parsons, Alice Humpal Petrik, Virgil D. Petrik, Elsie V. Petula, Dorothy Althoff Pies, Bernard Poppenga, Ida DeNeui Poppenga, Wilma Price, Karla Pritchard, Jan Bertsch Quenzer, Astrid Raad, Mary Ann Rager, LaVera Rall, John C. Ranek, Louise Ranek, Delbert Rawden, Dorothy Robbins, Kenneth Robbins, Lucille Robertson, Jeanne Biegler Roers, Helen Borwell Rossow, Thelma Bucholz Sayler, Leo Schatz, Freida Schuh, Ervin Schumacher, Johanna Schutz, Maxine Schuurmans, Tom Shonley, Sandy Sivertsen, H.T. Sly, Janet Fairchild Snow, Alpha R. Sorenson, South Dakota Department of Education and Cultural Affairs, South Dakota Historical Society, Dean J. Spader, Pat Speelman, Henry N. Stein, Eleanor Thompson, Mary Simonson Thompson, Steve Trim, Hazel Vennard, Cornie Neil Versteeg, Marjean Viksna, Frances Blessing Wagner, Henry L. Wells, Esther Bickel Werner, Darlene L. West, L. Westhoff, Karen Petersen White, Nellie M. Willurvent, Jerry W. Wilson, Joyce Michels Wittenhagen, and Dixie C. Young.

CONTENTS

They said they were never goin' back, it wasn't fair. For a while, Frank Sr. sat without comment. He chewed his food slowly, wiped his dark mustache, then looked at his freckly-faced son. "You never throwed one of them spitballs?" he asked. "Never?"

I was learning to write my name. My name, Ollie Not Stampede, was very long. We had a large map on the wall . . . and I saw the word *Asia*, short and easy to write. I very nicely finished my paper and wrote "Ollie Asia" on it. I couldn't understand why Miss Hines got so upset. I spent a lot of time at the chalkboard writing "Ollie Not Stampede" over and over again.

Little did the teacher know what was in store for her. The "leader," of course, knew exactly where the pit was dug and jumped over it, but the poor teacher didn't know, and down she dropped! You couldn't even see her after she fell in the hole in the snowbank.

Many a morning I had to scoop snow out of the school-room before the children would come and I would always build up a good fire, as they'd always be so cold, having to walk to school.

INTRODUCTION

RURAL LIFE IS THE LEGACY of the state of South Dakota, and at the foundation of this legacy is the one-room country school. Even today, long after most have disappeared, the one-room school remains the nation's most enduring symbol of education and the traditional values of Euro-American society. Rural school districts represent our smallest units of local government and have thrived or perished consistent with the amount of support offered them by local communities.

Despite the enduring significance of the one-room school and our expectation that this topic would spark public interest, the South Dakota Humanities Foundation did not fully anticipate the enthusiastic response of South Dakotans to the One-Room School project that we launched in the fall of 1997. When we asked for personal accounts of the one-room school experience, over a hundred individuals sent us stories. This impressive response reflects South Dakotans' high regard for the education they received in country schools. Most of the authors attended rural schools in South Dakota and are still living in this state. A few are former South Dakotas who now live in other states. Still fewer are South Dakotans who attended or taught in one-room schools in other states. We have arranged selections from these memoirs to mirror the school day and year and have also tried to follow the natural chronology of history within the separate thematic chapters.The setting of each anecdote in place and time follows each author's name.

This project is a collaborative venture that is truly open-ended. It began in the minds of six committee members—Rebecca Dunn, John Fiksdal, Mary Gederos, Michael Haug, Norma Wilson and Charles Woodard. Based on the memoirs submitted, Ken Robbins wrote the initial draft of the script for the reader's theatre. Dorothy Robbins did research and made initial contacts with communities to book the show. Clare Denton directed the premiere performances at Siston Theatre in Sisseton, July 18, 1998. Members of the cast were Sharon Prendergrast, June Kasyoki, Neal Nelson, Sandy Jaspers, Tom Prendergrast, Tressa Schmidt and John S. Nelson. Roger and Estelle Pearson played piano, and Wayne Knutson evaluated these performances.

This project has drawn from a number of sources, including the Country School Legacy Project, conducted by 23 researchers in 8 states—Colorado, Kansas, Nebraska, Nevada, Utah, Wyoming, North Dakota, and South Dakota—and sponsored by the Mountain Plains Library Association, the National Endowment for the Humanities and the Humanities Councils of the various states, as well as state and local libraries, agencies and interested citizens.

For thousands of years before the first Europeans entered Dakota Territory, the native Mandan, Hidatsa, Arikara, Dakota, Yankton and Teton peoples had educated their youth in the arts, philosophy, theology, ethics, moral conduct, and skills necessary to survive in a land which had sustained them so well that they considered it their mother. Charles Eastman, Zitkala-Sa, Luther Standing Bear, Ella C. Deloria, Beatrice Medicine, Virginia Driving Hawk Sneve, Elizabeth Cook-Lynn and many others have written of this educational process, which was passed on by the elders of America's original nations through oral tradition. This process of instruction was different in many ways from the schooling brought to the plains and prairies by the European settlers in the 19th century. Yet, both the Natives the Europeans realized the necessity of transmitting cultural values to their youth and of preparing them to be productive citizens who could work with others.

According to our research, the first school in the Euro-American mode, located in what is now South Dakota, was at the garrison of Old Fort Randall in the winter of 1857, and the teacher was a relative of Captain J. B. S. Todd, a land speculator in the Territory. The first public school in Dakota Territory was established in Bon Homme County in 1860. Nine students attended classes taught by Emma Bradford in a log cabin. The Territory's first legislative assembly enacted laws establishing a public school system in 1862. The first school to be permanently established was built in 1864 at the foot of Ravine Hill in Vermillion. Amos Shaw, a soldier in the Dakota Cavalry that built the school, taught the first classes.

James Foster, the first territorial superintendent of public instruction, directed the first teachers' institute at Elk Point the week of November 10, 1867. Twenty teachers attended. Since that time, teachers have continued to take advantage of the summer months to revitalize their teaching. In her memoir, Myrtle Hundstad Mortimer remembers a teacher institute held in the mid-1930s. Each summer since 1984, the South Dakota Humanities Council has funded teacher institutes at colleges and universities throughout the state, thus providing elementary and secondary school teachers the opportunity to enhance their knowledge in a variety of humanities disciplines.

Many of the state's earliest schools were conducted by Episcopal, Presbyterian, Congregational and Catholic missionaries for the education of Native American children. The United States government had encouraged these churches to build schools on Indian reservations. The first resident missionary in South Dakota, Rev. John P. Williamson, a Presbyterian, built a log house near the Yankton Agency at Greenwood in 1869. That building served as residence, church and school. The Episcopal Church, and to a lesser extent the Congregational and Catholic Churches, established many other missions during the following decade. Thereafter, church-run schools, often government-financed, were established in great numbers. Later in the 19th century, the federal government began to establish its own Indian schools, and many mission schools were sold or given to the government. By 1898, only one Protestant government-contract school remained in operation. Several Catholic schools continued to operate with financial support from tribal governments and mission organizations.

Schoolhouses were built before churches in many communities. By 1883, 426 teachers were employed in 385 public schools in Dakota Territory. Almost all were one-room schools with an average of fifteen students. In his introduction to *The Legacy of North Dakota's Country Schools*, Warren Henke says that the acquisition of "millions of acres of land from the federal government for educational and other public purposes was one of the greatest advantages of moving from territorial status to statehood." In the early days of statehood, South Dakotans believed that the revenue accrued from school lands would provide almost all the funds needed for public education.

The earliest teachers came to the Territory from the east, but by the end of the nineteenth century, many teachers were the sons and daughters of the first large rush of homesteaders.

When South Dakota joined the Union in 1889, there were 2,978 schools and 3,971 teachers in the state.

A 1913 state law required that Native American children be included in the census, and consequently that they be compelled to attend school. However, in 1915, the law was repealed. Thus, Indian parents living off the reservation did not have to send their children to school, which made it easier for some teachers, school board members and school administrators to discourage Native Americans from attending off-reservation schools. As many Native Americans sold their reservation land to white ranchers, public schools were gradually established on these lands, and Indian children living in the vicinity sometimes attended. Eventually, more than twenty day schools were established on the Pine Ridge Reservation. During the first decades of the twentieth century, most Indian children of western South Dakota started school speaking only the Lakota language.

For a large number of European immigrants who came to the state early in the century, learning to speak and write English in the schools was the first phase of the Americanization process. As a result of this wave of immigration, the number of one-teacher rural schools in South Dakota was at its peak at 5,011 in 1916. By 1918, there were almost as many one-room schools in the Midwest as there were in the rest of the nation.

However, the number of one-room schools declined as increased use of automobiles and improved roads allowed children to travel longer distances, which led to school consolidations and a decrease in the number of one-room schools. The operation of one-room schools has always required strong community support, and the economic and environmental struggles faced by South Dakotans during the Dust Bowl days presented such extreme difficulties that the period is indelibly impressed in the memories of those who lived through those hard times. In 1931-32 there were approximately 4,731 one-room schools in South Dakota. The flight from rural to urban areas that resulted from the Great Depression also contributed to consolidation and a decrease in the number of rural schools. By 1943-44, only 3,599 one-room schools remained.

The teacher was a major factor in the success or failure of the one-room school. Often poorly educated and poorly paid, living in unheated rooms and required to do the custodial and maintenance work of the school, teachers were, at the same time, the primary role models for their students. In 1937-38, the average annual salary for teachers in urban schools was $1,952 nationwide. In rural schools, it was $864. The total amount spent per pupil in urban schools was $100, compared to $66 per pupil in rural schools.

In 1940, only seven states required four years of preparation for teaching after completion of high school. Ten required three years, seventeen required two years, and the remaining fourteen required one year or less after high school. In seven states, high school graduates could be hired for a limited number of years if they passed a state board examination.

Nationwide, the number of one-teacher schools decreased 88% from 1918-1959. In 1960 there were 23,695 one-teacher schools in the United States, one of every four public schools. Almost a tenth of these, 2,338, were in South Dakota. By 1981, there were just over 1,000 one-room schools in the entire United States, and still, roughly a tenth of these were in South Dakota. Between 1974 and 1983, more than a hundred one-teacher schools closed in South Dakota, the number declining from 230 to 104. At the end of the century, South Dakota is still home to fifty elementary schools with enrollments of fewer than twenty students. Some of these are public; others are private. Most are located in remote areas and provide an important service to children and their families, who would otherwise have to travel distances of sixty miles or more to the next closest school.

Although the one-room school experiences reflected upon in the following memoirs are for the most part positive, it is evident that the experience was sometimes fraught with difficulty andfrustration. The harsh climate and the hard life on the prairie often forced schools to limit their terms, and children were often kept home to do the work that was vital to the survival of their families.

Discipline not only trained youngsters in skills, but forced them to conform to social expectations. Immigrants and Native Americans were forced to abandon their first languages and adopt English in the classroom. How distressing that as a seven-year-old Lakota schoolgirl, Ollie (Not Stampede) Napesni, whose memoir follows, was punished for creatively giving herself a new name, *Asia*. That she should have chosen to name herself for the continent that is home to India, the country for which Native Americans were misnamed by Columbus, is both ironic and significant. Her self-naming might have initiated an enlightening intellectual discussion, instead of the tedious, repetitious exercise that only caused resentment.

Had Lakota, German, Norwegian, Czech, and Danish-speaking students been encouraged to share their first language skills with English-speaking students, a bilingual classroom could have evolved that would have set the students on a course toward better intercultural relations and a broader base of knowledge. Unfortunately, this is a lesson our society has yet to learn. At the end of the twentieth century, the study of languages other than English has become so devalued that few rural schools, other than those on the Indian reservations or in the Hutterite colonies, provide students with the opportunity to learn to think and speak from another cultural perspective.

Despite the difficulties that still exist in rural schools, the memoirs we received express, on the whole, a spirit of community and an appreciation for the one-room school experience. These stories and statements make it very apparent that the educational process works best when teachers and students and the community of which they are a part have mutual respect and rely on and learn from one another.

Though many unused one-room schoolhouses have fallen to ruin, some do remain intact, because citizens have taken the initiative to restore them. For example, one-room schoolhouses can be visited at Friends of the Middle Border Museum in Mitchell, at Prairie Village in Madison, on the Augustana College Campus in Sioux Falls, at the Huron State Fairgrounds and at Keystone, DeSmet and Yankton. Such school restorations can stimulate the memories of their former students, and they can help those who never had the experience to better understand what it was like to teach and learn in such an environment.

At the end of the century, there are still a number of one-room schoolhouses being used for the purposes for which they were intended. The largest number of rural schools in 1997 were in Meade District, which had seven elementary schools with fewer than twenty students. That same year there were six elementary schools in the Haakon District with five to twenty students each. Alfalfa Valley Elementary School, with the largest enrollment, held classes in an old schoolhouse and a trailer.

Even the smallest of rural schools have computers in the classroom. Most rural teachers have aides, and the South Dakota Humanities Council's Speakers Bureau and Resource Center and the South Dakota Arts Council's Artist-in-Residence Program offer many resources for expanding the offerings of these schools. However, small rural schools, like schools everywhere, still need the financial support of their communities in order to utilize these resources.

This book is not intended to provide a definitive representation of the country school, but rather to stimulate further research, community discussions and storytelling, and ultimately to enhance the public's understanding of the essential values and content that have been taught in our schools. We hope that all facets of this reconsideration of the one-room school experience will help the people of South Dakota to assess the development and the future of education in our state.

Making selections for this book was difficult. We wish it were possible for us to print all the memoirs, because we learned from all of them.

These are the voices of the one-room country school.

Norma C. Wilson and Charles L. Woodard

PRELUDE

I WENT TO SCHOOL IN LEOLA.

I remember it as if it was yesterday. It was 1911 and I was five years old. The starting grade was the Primer. The room accommodated the Primer, First Grade and Second Grade. My sister Lola was in Second Grade.

The teacher had a poem written on the blackboard which I shall never forget. Of course she had to read it to us, but it was stamped in my memory forever:

Fleecy white sails spreading
  While shines the sun bright.
Gleaming and glowing
  With silvery light.
Where do you anchor
  When storm clouds come nigh?
Is there a harbor
  To which you fly?

Perhaps this is why I became a poet.

Alpha Bell Sorensen, Leola Public School,
McPherson County, SD, 1911

I GRADUATED FROM NORTHERN STATE TEACHERS COLLEGE in the spring of 1932, after attending classes for one nine-month term. I had my practice teaching experience in a two-room, two-teacher rural school a short distance from Aberdeen. I was then certified to teach in any rural school in South Dakota. Certified, yes! Qualified, no! I had never been inside a country school.

My brother took me and my possessions to the schoolhouse on a warm Labor Day afternoon. I was to live in a "teacherage," which was a corner at one end of the schoolroom.

When we approached the buildings, we saw several cars and some horses. Oh, Boy! A welcoming committee? As we approached, the door was open and we heard singing, church songs. A woman came out and introduced herself; then I was invited to come in and was introduced. She said, "This is the new teacher." There was silence as I was inspected; then I finally introduced myself and received a few smiles and nods. Talk about nervous! I think my face was all shades of red. I was waiting for someone to say something, and finally it dawned on me that I had interrupted their worship service. The man who seemed to be in charge asked me to join them, as they were almost ready to close the service. After about a half hour of reading, everyone stood and prayed. I was thankful to hear the "Amen." Then he said, "We will close singing "God Be With You 'Til We Meet Again"—all five verses! I joined in the singing, but I had my eyes on the little building out back that seemed so far from the schoolhouse and I wondered how soon I could get to it.

Everyone there said something to me before leaving, and I tried to be gracious. One couple stayed to help unload so my brother could get back to Mobridge. It was a shock to see my living quarters. The walls of the tiny room were just partitions, open at the top for ventilation. There was a small window, but no curtain and no place to hang clothes. There was a small stand or cupboard, a chair and a folding couch with no mattress! The woman who had introduced me laughed and said she had stored the mattress at their house, as mice had built a home in it. Good Grief! Mice! I took time to inspect every corner of the building; then this woman invited me to spend the night with them, and she would take me to school the next morning, and would come again after school to help me get settled.

After a hearty breakfast, my hostess took me, a lunch for the day, and oh yes, the mattress, to school.

About 8:30 a.m. my pupils started coming, eighteen of them, all sizes and all grades, of course, and two little girls who could not speak English. The one seventh grade girl was not at all shy, and she was a blessing to me throughout the term, as she could speak German.

We spent all forenoon getting acquainted and had a long, leisurely lunch hour. In the afternoon, we made a map of the area and located each student's home. This was a great, first-day activity, that I also used in other schools.

Freida Schuh, Landeau School,
Corson County, SD, 1932-33

THERE IS IN LATE SUMMER, in a country schoolyard, a quiet softness like no other. It is the afternoon before the first day of school. The grass is scrunchy from the hot Dakota sun. A few bumblebees are gathering the last bit of summer's sweetness. Lacy white butterflies flutter about like little girls in white dresses. Cows graze lazily in a nearby pasture and the distant caw of a crow signals that cooler weather will soon come. A curious little striped gopher stands tall to see who is intruding on his summer domain. Even the little fiddlers in the grass draw their bows a bit slower.

All of this, the lull before the storm.

Inside, wonderful smells provide the ambiance. New paint, fresh oil cloth, soap on the wash stand, well-scrubbed desks, new books, crayons and pencils. Later, little children smelling of breakfasts of pancakes and bacon and a bit of barnyard on their shoes from early morning chores will line up their dinner buckets, laden with over-ripe fruit and peanut butter and jelly sandwiches. If the day grows cold, smoke from the wood-burning stove will join the olfactory symphony.

The eternal green border with its large cursive alphabet looms above the blackboard and the dreary rolled-up maps. The handbell on the teacher's desk sits in royal command. The recitation bench waits to hold court for little minds. Directly across, the piano and hopefully a phonograph are attempts to add a little culture.

The stage is set. The teacher rings the bell and the little actors file in and take their places. The school year has begun.

Mary Ann Rager, Howard District 30 and
Hillview District 12 Schools, Yankton County, SD, 1946-50

Characters and Their Roles

ON MY FIRST DAY OF SCHOOL, I returned home to announce that I would someday be a teacher because all a teacher did was ask questions and the children had to answer them.

On my first day of teaching, this life-long illusion self-destructed in 30 seconds. Much to my surprise, when 42 question marks looked me square in the eye, I found that the teacher also had to know all the answers and how to make a fire in a coal or wood stove, and how to prepare an adequate lunch, and how to provide entertainment for all sorts of occasions, and how to crowd all the subjects into one day!

I learned that in a rural school, kindergarten through eighth grade, I would have to be nurse, doctor, mother, counselor, cook, custodian, babysitter, referee, and diplomat living on promises.

On that first day, I was amazed at the size of my pupils, especially the boys; I wasn't sure whether to date them or teach them, but I remembered that my contract specifically mentioned teaching, so I set about my task. There followed one of the longest days of my life. The clock literally stood still. It gave very little boost to my already deflated ego when I overheard one of the six-foot boys whisper, "She'll never make it!"

I learned that I must always set a good example because I might be the only Bible some children would ever read. I learned that reasoning with a child is fine, if you can reach the child's reason without destroying your own.

I learned that every class contains the following: wigglers; dreamers; numerous bathroom-goers; the town crier who shouts out all the answers (90% wrong) and announces everything that has or is about to happen; the spiller; the crayon eaters; the hyperactive child, who seems to be in every part of the room at once; the wrecking crew members who shake up the entire room whenever they leave their desks; the nibblers who nibble away on their own pencils and crayons and on the teacher's patience; the shy, timid child for whom we are very thankful, once in a while, but who may have the deepest problem.

I learned that I must be reliable, socially mature (but not too), intelligent, religious, generous, patient (if the $45 per month salary checks arrived "Funds Unavailable") and retain enough humor to face outraged parents.

Nevertheless, I enjoyed those days, and I hope that along the way I scattered a few seeds of knowledge along the flowery path of learning. Maybe we were lucky, we who endured those early hardships, for we learned resourcefulness, and since we had no help or aid, we cultivated the inner strength to evaluate our own problems and courage to work them out before they worked us over.

Given the same situations again we would do it all over, because a teacher dispenses magic and sells futures. Dreams are her stock in trade. Secretly, we would admit we had the greatest job in the world, because we held history in our hands.

Mary Magirl Dougherty, Emporia School,
Holt County, SD, 1911-12

IN THOSE DAYS TEACHERS were treated with great respect and were expected to be role models for the children.

Lily P. Hanson Kruse, Bennet School, Haakon County &
Cane Creek School, Pine Ridge Reservation, SD, 1932-36

IT WAS A WEEK AFTER MY 18TH BIRTHDAY when at 8:45 a.m. I faced ten eager, suntanned faces of children aged six to fourteen in a single-room, red brick schoolhouse in Bon Homme County. I was about to start my teaching career. I was "well prepared" by ten weeks of college in courses like "Rural School Management" and "Arithmetic I." A permit granting me the legal authority to teach in a rural school for one year rested in my shiny new, brown leather briefcase.

A week or two before that opening day, I made a trip out to that schoolhouse to become acquainted with the facilities and make preparations for the start of school. I had never set foot in a rural school before in my life. I stopped at the farm of the board treasurer to get the key to the building, and then I was on my own—no orientation tour of the building, no one to give me a briefing on the children.

As I checked out the school, I found a built-in book closet where the textbooks were stored and I checked them over. Other than knowing that the books with the big print went to the smallest kids and those with smaller print went to older kids, I wasn't sure which books went to which children.

The worry of resolving the problem of which book went to which student was still on my mind as I drove out to the school on that opening day. But after I introduced myself and welcomed the kids back to school, the solution to the problem came to me.

I simply turned to Shirley, the eighth grade girl, and asked her to pass out the books. Shirley saw to it that each child received the books he or she needed. Shirley's eight years of experience in that building came to be a valuable asset to me as the school year progressed.

Virgil D. Petrik, Vlasak School District 27,
Bon Homme County, SD, 1949-50

I HAD BEEN THE ONLY STUDENT IN MY GRADE for all six years and longed for a classmate. Imagine my excitement when we heard that there was a large, new family in the neighborhood who would be attending our school. Finally, there would be enough kids to play "Fox and Goose," "Pump, Pump, Pull Away," and have a real ballgame.

The first day of school arrived, and I was there bright and early. I loved going to school and seldom missed a day; now the great possibility of a classmate made it even more exciting.

Well, my "classmate" dream evaporated when seven Leistras (all with names starting with the letter D) showed up—and not one of them was in the seventh grade!

I was disappointed for a while, but still enjoyed the new students. I even had a childhood crush on one of the handsome Leistra boys.

Norma Moller, Mullivan School,
Aurora County, SD, 1947

I WAS THE THIRD BORN IN A FAMILY OF SIX CHILDREN. We lived eighteen miles from any town (so you would call it God's Country) and when I was ready for school the school board in this township was obligated to open the Norfolk School because we now had three children attending. My two older brothers had previously had to board in town at Grandma's house so they could attend school. Our school was one room with a cot in the corner for the teacher to sleep on.

After a couple of years of just being the three of us, a family of good Catholics moved in, and just about every year we had one more kid in school.

Seemed like we never were sure we had a teacher until the day before school started because of our school being so far out in the country.

I graduated from the 8th grade with two other gals. The three of us got to go into Onida for an 8th grade graduation banquet. For this big occasion I got my first pair of earrings and a new dress.

Betty Rupkalves Herron, Norfolk School,
Sully County, SD, Late 1945-50

W e a r a n d T e a r

ONE OF THE WORST THINGS ABOUT SCHOOL was keeping up with the laundry. We had to be real careful with our school clothes and had to change them when we got home from school so we could wear them another day. We did not have modern equipment to launder our clothes efficiently. We had a summer kitchen and we had to heat our water on an old cookstove. We did a lot of hand washing, and hauling of water was not easy either.

Hazel Vennard, Newdale School 43,
Clay County, SD, 1926-34

7

IN THE WINTER, BOTH BOYS AND GIRLS often wore long underwear and bib overalls to school. We wore long cotton stockings underneath and 4-buckle overshoes in the winter. My mother sewed lots of our clothing. One time she made us bloomers out of cotton flour sacks. They covered our bottoms well, but a girl in school discovered the X's across the seats of our pants and started teasing my sister and I about our flour-sack pants. We hated her because her mom bought her nice pink rayon panties. She was the same girl whose mother didn't force her to wear long cotton socks held up by garter belts over long underwear nearly as long as our mom did. More than once I rolled the socks down the minute I got to school and rolled the underwear up into untidy bunches at the top. Each of us usually had a school dress and a chore outfit for work at home. Dresses were handed down, so often the same one would show up on several sisters, as the years went by. Girls didn't wear slacks to school unless it was terribly cold. Then they wore them under their dresses so they could be taken off indoors.

Phylis Brunken, Law School,
Douglas County, SD, 1934-42

ONE FALL DAY WE WALKED TO SCHOOL. After I got inside the schoolhouse and removed my coat, I realized I didn't have on a dress (My mother had made one of my old dresses into a "slip" by cutting out the sleeves and collar). Before any of the children noticed it, I ran home, crying all the way. My mother helped me put on a dress and I ran back. The kids wondered why I was so late, but I never told them.

Johanna Schutz, Burma School District 69, 1930-35

THE STUDENTS HAD BEEN DISMISSED after their noon lunches had been eaten to go outside to play on the slide and swings. I was detained for a few minutes. Just as I was getting ready to go outside, I heard a noisy bunch of children scramble back into the building. One pudgy, little red-haired fifth-grade girl came into the schoolroom with that "Now what will I do?" look on her face.

She had been at the top of the slide, and other children behind her had said, "Hurry Up, Get Going!" Well, hurry she had! She had hit the top of the slide with a take-off motion that had fluffed her skirt out like an umbrella. Her skirt had hooked over the top of the hand-bars at the top of the slide, and half of it had been torn off and left hanging on the hand-bars. Having no telephone to call her mother, we had to improvise some way to keep her looking proper for the rest of the day. None of us had a needle or thread, but with a lot of safety pins, we pinned her up like you put a diaper on a baby, with the front of the skirt pinned to the remnants of the back.

Shirley E. Juracek, Pershing School District 50,
Yankton County, SD, 1971-72

DURING WORLD WAR II rubber was scarce, and so elastic in underwear was made of a synthetic material. Women, especially school teachers, did not wear slacks. One day as our teacher stood opening the door, her underwear elastic broke and there she stood, "So Em bare assed."

Lorraine Crouch, Wilson School District 4, Oceola, IA, 1945

MANY A MORNING I HAD TO SCOOP SNOW out of the schoolroom before the children would come and I would always build up a good fire, as they'd always be so cold, having to walk to school. One morning one of the younger boys was late getting to school, and he insisted on keeping his overshoes on, and being it was so near recess time, I didn't press the issue, but during recess I insisted he remove the overshoes, and with much hesitation he did, so I found to my dismay that he didn't even have socks on his feet, and of course they were frozen. I immediately got busy to thaw out those feet, wrapped them in rags and put anklets of mine on them, and wrote a note home that the boy wasn't to return to school without something besides overshoes on his feet.

Ruth I. Foster, Thorpe School, Perkins County, SD, 1938-39

To and From School

WHAT I REMEMBER MOST is the long, two-mile walk my older brothers, my two sisters and I took morning and afternoon, regardless of the weather, unless my father thought it was too cold or rainy for survival.

We would cut through the cattle yard and across fields for the first mile, in muddy weather, probably wearing the same buckle-overshoes we had worn in the milking barn. A rock crossing spanning a small creek led to a barbed-wire fence which enclosed the pasture in which the bull that we had been warned of so often roamed.

If we felt brave and were short of precious time (as happened quite often), we might take another shortcut through the yard of a farmer who was known (so we had been told) to sic his dogs on unwelcome visitors. We suspected that this elderly man didn't mind our comings and goings, but we kept a wary eye out for his oversized collies.

Finally on the unimproved dirt road, we really hurried, swinging our tin syrup pails to the uneven beat of our five pairs of feet. Usually playtime would have to wait until morning and afternoon recesses and the short noon hour.

We could dawdle on the return trip. Our brothers usually got well ahead, but waited for us, because no one was in a hurry to start the evening chores. Our worn shoes would scuff the soft black dust in the road into miniature storm clouds. In the fall there'd be time to pick coneflowers for Mom in exchange for the cookies she would have waiting for us. In the winter there was time for making snow angels, and in the spring, time for gathering fragrant blossoms from the wild plum and chokecherry bushes crowding the ditches.

Not until the doting parents of a neighboring eighth grader gave their son a coupe of his own to drive to school did we gratefully give up our long walk. By then there were only three of us to crowd in with our pint-sized driver. And on the unimproved roads we had in those days, those drives were experiences in themselves!

Maxine Schuurmans, Koupal School District 24,
Bon Homme County, SD, 1932-40

MY SCHOOL WAS THREE MILES from the Fough Ranch, so I needed a horse to ride. Mr. Fough didn't know I could ride, so he gave me a nearly dead horse. This horse was so slow that every day I was afraid I would be late getting to school. Many a time I felt like turning him loose and losing him in the Slim Buttes where I was teaching. Arriving at school, I had to chop wood, start a fire in the coal furnace, and get a pail of fresh water at the hand pump. The pupils and I brought pail lunches.

Finally Mr. Fough felt sorry for me riding that bony old horse, and he lent me his favorite riding horse, a jet black mare. Now I got to school nearly before I started—that was a running horse! One stormy night I frightened her with my lunch pail while getting on, and she bucked me off and took off running over the hill. I had started to walk when I heard pounding hooves getting closer, and don't you know, my horse had come back for me! I gave her a hug and a couple of love pats, then got back on and we headed for the ranch. I kept this little secret between me and my horse.

Florence Lewton Gunn, Maltby School,
Perkins County, SD, 1930-31

MY FIRST YEAR OF TEACHING, I was 19 years old. There were two families living on Bridges Creek about three miles apart, so they got together and built a 10' x 10' shack for a schoolhouse. I lived three and a half miles away, so I rode horseback on "Old Jake" to school each day, sometimes against a cold north wind.

One of my last days of school I was in a hurry and forgot to tighten the cinch. In the twinkling of an eye, I was under the belly of a wildly kicking horse. When I saw those hooves fly over my head I decided to let go. He bucked and kicked until he was exhausted and stopped some ways away, scared to death. I finally caught him and got the saddle back up. He hadn't broken the cinch. I got home safely, but "Old Jake" would never let me ride him again.

Lily P. Hanson Kruse, Bennett School,
Haakon County, SD, 1932

14

ONE WINTER, I SPENT SIX WEEKS or maybe even longer without seeing anyone but the children I taught. So I was yearning for adult conversation. One Friday, after the children had left, I glimpsed the county snowplow opening the highway, so immediately I packed a small overnight case and struck off to reach the plowed-out highway, heading north, northwest to the home of some friends. Walking wasn't too bad as long as I could follow the highway before it became dark. But suddenly it was dark, and I had to leave the highway and head across country. I was told later there were many open wells that I could have fallen into, and no one would have had any idea of what had become of the teacher. But God was with me, because even with often plunging into snow over waist deep, I made it to the home of my friends. What shocked expressions came on their faces when I knocked on their door. The dog hadn't announced my coming so they were truly surprised to see me standing on their step. I had walked over eleven miles that night, and the next day my muscles told me they had been abused. I was young and yes, no doubt a bit foolish, but I felt I just had to get to civilization, or at least see faces other than the school children's. As much as I loved them, I needed to see other people.

Ruth I. Foster, Thorpe School,
Perkins County, SD, 1938-39

15

The Schoolhouse

THE SCHOOLROOM WAS ALWAYS FRESH AND CLEAN to go back to on the first day. The mothers always got together and cleaned the school well before class began each fall. After that, it was the teacher's responsibility to keep the floors and blackboards clean.

It seemed that no school was without pictures of President Lincoln and President Washington, and usually there was a big clock between them at the front of the room. There was also a learning chart, which consisted of several sheets of paper, 3' x 4'. A picture was on the top half, and the words were on the bottom half. It was used for first grade reading lessons. The chart hung by a cord and was attached to a stand or from a hook. The sheets were flipped over and hung on the back side in preparation for the next lesson.

The maps were large, about 4' x 5'. How fascinating they were! The country you wanted to look at could be pulled down like a window shade and then rolled back up into a container.

Irene Hansen, Myhre School,
Fallon County, MT, 1922-30

THE LARGE MAIN ROOM OF OUR SCHOOL had board floors. The walls and ceilings were a dove-gray, decorative tin, with scrolls and tiny floral designs. The tin came down the walls, two-thirds of the way. Narrow brown oak strips of wood were nailed together, completing the wall coverings.

There were six narrow, eight-foot tall windows, three on the west and three on the east sides of the school room. Fly specks and buzzing wasps on the windows were normal.

Students' desks were sized according to how big they were. All were oak or walnut with black iron ornamental frames and legs. The seats were wooden, with spaces under them to hold books and school supplies.

The desk parts had grooves to hold pens and pencils. Round holes held messy ink wells. Heaven help a little girl who had long braids. If she had a young boy seated behind her, he spent more time trying to dip the ends of her braids in the ink bottle than he did studying or counting fly specks on the ceiling or windows.

Rozella Bracewell, Riggs School,
Meade County, SD, 1927-34

I STAYED WITH LOU AND BESS HEATHERSHAW on the Seven Springs Ranch, just down the hill from the schoolhouse. Their place was like an oasis with all that water, while the surrounding area was having a drought. The schoolhouse was built of cottonwood logs chinked with cement. In the winter we pulled our desks closer to the stove and managed to keep warm. We had a water bucket and each child had his own cup. To get water we would go down to the creek, push the leaves aside and dip up a bucket of the most beautiful crystal clear water. There were six pupils: Harry Damson, Calvin Shangreau, Darrell Powers, Carolyn and Ethelyn Ferguson, and Darwin Meili. It was a public school, and Indians and whites could attend.

Lily P. Hanson Kruse, Cane Creek School,
Pine Ridge Indian Reservation, 1935-36

MY SECOND SCHOOL was perhaps the oldest school in the county. It was small and drafty and crowded. I had ten Indian children and nine white children in a room so tiny there was not room for a recitation bench. There were four rows of desks, with the two outside rows against the walls. Those pupils were always cold. As skinny as I was in those days, I had to go sideways up the aisle to get to the blackboard in the front of the room. The windows were all on the north side where one row of desks were.

Winifred Bertrand Fawcett, Bridge School,
Potter County, SD, 1934-44

18

EDDY SCHOOL HAD THE ONE LARGE ROOM typical of the one room schools. Two cloakrooms, two storage rooms and a full basement completed the schoolhouse layout. The coal-burning furnace was directly under a large grate in the classroom floor. The basement provided a play area on those days when weather forced us to stay in. At the top of the stairs going into the classroom was a mezzanine that contained the bucket of drinking water. The older boys would walk to Grandpa Borkowski's to fill the water bucket. The large window gave the teacher a full view to make sure they didn't waste any time.

The furnace grate was always covered with wet coats, hats and overshoes in the winter, and the school always smelled of wet wool or cotton. Sometimes the fire would be so hot that the top of the furnace would glow red. If you stood on the grate too long, grids would be burnt into the soles of your shoes.

Next to the large windows was an activity table for crafts. We could color, make things from wet paper or pipe cleaners, or just make a mess. There was always a large jar of white paste at the end of the table. Roger ate paste. I learned later that Roger was killed along the side of the road. Roger ate paste and was my friend at Eddy School.

Gerald Matson, Eddy School,
Jerauld County, SD, 1946-51

I STARTED TEACHING IN 1953. This was in Cottonwood School, a one-room schoolhouse located 9 miles north of White River. Water was hauled from a well and dumped into the cistern near the schoolhouse. From this cistern we got our drinking water. I had a rope tied to the handle of a bucket which I lowered into the cistern to get the water. We had no electricity. If we needed a light, we used a kerosene lamp. The schoolhouse had windows on the west side, so the pupils faced the north. The theory then was that the light should come from the left.

Thelma Bucholz Sayler, Cottonwood School District,
Mellette County, SD, 1953-54

I STARTED FIRST GRADE in District 42 in 1960, thirty years after my father and uncles had attended the same school. I was always fascinated that my father's name, Rolf, was carved in the wood along the cloakroom hooks.

I went back to District 42 a few years ago. There were still some books on the library shelves with titles that I recognized from long ago, and I felt like a giant next to the very low chalkboards that at one time had seemed just the right height. I went back to the cloakroom, and sure enough, there was my dad's name, just as he had carved it back in the thirties, still easily distinguishable on the wood where coats had once hung.

Janet Hovey Johnson, Sterling School District 42,
Brookings County, SD, 1960-65

The Outhouse

TOILETS WERE TWO OUTDOOR WOODEN PRIVIES, one for the boys and one for the girls. Each was off-limits to the opposite sex.

The seat had two round holes over a deep, oblong hole in the ground. Pages from Montgomery Ward and Sears Roebuck catalogues provided toilet paper. In some, calendars were on a wall, and sometimes a pictorial hanging of the Lord's prayer was on the other wall.

Because feces froze up into peaked mountains in the winter, it was necessary to sprinkle generous amounts of lime over it.

In the spring and fall, it was not uncommon to find a large bullsnake stretched out on the ledge down in the hole.

Rozella Bracewell, Riggs School,
Meade County, SD, 1927-34

THE OUTHOUSE WAS USED FALL, WINTER AND SPRING. Students ventured out during the winter only if very necessary. One day a couple of my second graders could not brave the cold and preferred to remain sitting in their accidents. No one wanted to sit near them because they smelled too bad.

Both students eventually grew up and graduated from the country school and went on to high school and college. They are now professional men, probably not recalling their tutor and the odors she tried to overlook as she helped them become better students.

There were other such accidents. Some of them could be remedied by standing over the furnace grate to dry out. Other accidents could not be remedied until the students returned home at the end of the day. On those days I sat as far from my students as I could as I helped them learn their spelling, arithmetic and reading.

Shirley Benz, Springdell School,
Deuel County, SD, 1942-48

THE 7TH AND 8TH GRADE BOYS found great fun in pulling outhouse pranks, like the time they herded a cow into the girls' toilet. The toilet was big enough for two seats and no more. There was a narrow door on one side and no way to turn the poor critter around.

The teacher made one of the guilty parties remove the cow. To do that he had to squeeze in behind her, step across the two seats, and persuade her to back out the door.

Then there was that one wintry Monday morning when we got to school and found to our dismay that "the big boys" had pulled off another one. They had worked hard on the project either Friday night after school or Sunday after church. Two huge snowballs, each big enough to be the bottom of a large snowman, were perched, one on each closed seat lid, inside the girls' outhouse. They had rolled them up and carried them into the toilet, and then added size to them by packing on more snow until neither snowball would fit through the door to be removed. The snow was packed and frozen so hard that it took those boys all morning to chisel those snowballs to a removable size, and they had to spend their noon and afternoon recesses catching up on their morning school work.

I wouldn't want to give up indoor plumbing just so my children could experience homemade fun the outhouse way, but it is a shame they miss out on so many good jokes!

Carol Boies, Dixon School, Gregory County, SD, 1966

❖

Banking the Fire

ADELLA AMELIA OLSON was born to John W. Olson and Anne G. Olson on July 4, 1866 in Walworth County, Wisconsin. With her parents and two sisters she came to Union County, Dakota Territory in 1869. At the age of sixteen, she began to teach the first term of school taught in Spink District School #49.

There was no schoolhouse in the district as yet, so a small room at the north end of a lumber lean-to built on the west side of a substantial house of hewn logs was utilized for the purpose of keeping school. The house was the home of a school officer with whose family she was to board. A small heater was placed in the room. Wood was the only fuel. It was brought from the timber along the Missouri River, 14 to 16 miles away, so fire could not be kept overnight.

In the mornings, Adella stood back, allowing the pupils who had come through the cold of a severe January to gather about the stove. Her feet were numb to the knees each forenoon, and eventually severe chillbains resulted. Infection set in; she was taken home. After three weeks, a physician was called. But the infection had gone into her circulation. She passed away May 1, 1883.

Anonymous, Spink District School #49,
Union County, SD, 1883

OUR HEATING SYSTEM WAS CRUDE. Every morning I would start the fire in the big-belly stove, carry out the ashes, and do the janitor work. One farmer delivered some corn cobs to help start the fire. Soon the mice moved in, and another chore was to set the mousetraps daily. There was a lot of excitement in the classroom if a mouse was found in a desk drawer.

Esther Werner,
Campbell County, SD, 1930s

ON A FRIDAY IN MARCH OF 1930 our rural school burned to the ground, and all of us students were in the school when the fire started. I was in the third grade at Sterling District Number 42, Brookings County. The reason that I know it was Friday was that part of Friday was reserved for art, and my complete art work was lost in the fire.

Due to the fairly mild weather, the fire had gone out in the furnace. Earlier in the day, the teacher had the students stack a load of kindling wood in the basement. Because of a lack of supervision, students stacked the wood too close to the furnace.

Later in the afternoon there was a chill in the schoolroom, and the teacher sent one of the older boys to the basement to build a fire in the furnace. He poured the kerosene to get the fire going.

At first, we were not too concerned with the excessive smoke. The schoolhouse was then evacuated, but the teacher allowed those of us who had left our coats and dinner pails behind to re-enter the building to retrieve those items.

Our farmhouse was just a half mile from the schoolhouse. My two brothers and I hurried home, where my father had a team of horses hooked up to a bobsled in preparation for evening chores. The hired man, our father, and we kids all got in the bobsled and hurried back to the burning schoolhouse. The hired man shoveled snow down through the basement window, but it was to no avail.

Because of the lack of communication at that time, word of the fire did not spread until parents came after their children at dismissal time. The Bruce Fire Department finally came, but with only a hand-held fire extinguisher. By that time, the building was totally consumed by fire.

One of the boys who attended the school was crying, and most of us couldn't figure that out. Among the rest of us boys there was a secret rejoicing. No schoolhouse–no school! However, it didn't work out that way. The Bruce School generously donated one schoolroom and necessary textbooks. Monday morning, our classes were functioning normally in Bruce. We never missed a minute of school.

Rolf N. Hovey, Sterling District 42 School,
Brookings County, SD, 1930

DURING THE 1930S, we burned coal in the stove in the front and center of the room. It was kept in the coal bin that was partitioned off from the entry-cloak room. One winter someone regularly stole the coal once a week. Every morning we would look in the coal room to see if any coal was missing. We could usually tell if someone had shoveled coal out during the night by looking on the ground under the west window.

Evelyn Myers Sharping, Swanson School,
Brule County, SD, 1931-39

ON MONDAY, TUESDAY AND WEDNESDAY MORNINGS, the thermometer was at forty degrees below zero Fahrenheit. Thursday and Friday were only eighteen below in the morning. Not all the homes had telephones, and I was worried that some pupils would come to school and freeze if the school wasn't warm. So I walked that mile each day, clad in a fur-lined cap, coat, and the mittens my mother had lined for me, plus leggings, a scarf, and high-buckle overshoes, since there was snow. No kids came all week, so I lit the heater, warmed myself, let the fire die out, prepared the stove so it could be quickly started the next morning, and went home.

There was plenty of coal and wood for kindling and an ax for splitting the kindling. Once a piece of wood flew up and broke my glasses. This necessitated flagging the train at a nearby grain elevator, going to Aberdeen and getting new lenses. Fortunately this happened on a Friday.

Myrtle Hundstad Mortimer,
Edmunds County, SD, 1932-33

THE SCHOOL BOARD should have warned me that I needed to come to my job with an axe because one was not provided. They did well to fill the coal bin with good, big chunks of coal and scrap lumber for kindling. But neither coal nor wood would fit in the stove. I solved this problem by taking the coal out to huge rocks in the yard and dropping it on the rocks and ducking quickly so I wouldn't get coal splinters in my eyes. I propped the wood against the cement step and jumped on it several times to get it small enough for kindling. I tried banking the fire to keep a little heat in the stove till morning, but oh, oh, those cold, cold Monday mornings. Not once did anyone start the fire for me. Well, after all, I was contracted to teach their school for the princely sum of $60 a month.

Winifred Bertrand Fawcett, Bridge School,
Potter County, SD, 1943-44

MY FORTY-THREE YEARS OF TEACHING country schools in South Dakota began near Academy, in Charles Mix County. My first school was five and a half miles from my parents' home. I rode horseback or else walked. During the bad weather I stayed with a family a half mile from the school.

A pot-bellied stove furnished the heat. I gathered kindling to start the fire. During the cold weather before I left school at the end of the day, I'd bank the fire. To bank the fire, I'd put coal on it and ashes over the coal. By doing this, the stove would be warm the next morning. Sometimes it would be too hot and the next morning I'd see that some of the crayons had melted.

Ruth Graves Ellis, McKay and Heaton Schools,
Charles Mix County, SD, 1940

EVERY MORNING, either the teacher or some of the older kids would stoke up the furnace which was in the basement. The school room was heated by radiant heat from the floor register above the furnace.

One cold December morning in 1943, little Bobby, who was in first grade, came to school and said his mother told him he needed to stay inside during recess and lunch time because he had a toothache.

On this same morning after the furnace was going really good and classes had been in session for some time, someone noticed smoke coming from the floor register. The teacher ran downstairs to check on things and came rushing back up telling us our school building was on fire. She quickly sent all the young children outside while the older students helped her carry books and other valuables outside.

But little Bobby refused to go out. He insisted that his mother told him he had to stay inside because of a toothache. We were all concerned about Bobby, and after quite a struggle his older sister did convince him to go outside.

Leo Schatz, Farmer's School District 2,
McIntosh County, ND, December 1943

ENTERING THOSE DARK ROOMS AT 7:30 A.M., daylight savings time and fumbling your way around to put down your lunch pail and your bag of homework and papers that were corrected the night before was a feat in itself—let alone getting down those creaky dark stairs to the furnace room.

I had become well acquainted with that routine in other schools where I had taught, but in this particular school I had many eerie, spine-chilling fears on those dark winter mornings.

Every Thursday morning I noted that someone had situated himself by that warm furnace sometime during the previous night. He had left his rear-end indentation in the tub of ashes that I had to carry out. Nothing else was disturbed anywhere in the building, so I believe that all he wanted to do was enter a warm furnace room on a dark, winter night, perhaps after having been to a night club nearby. Maybe he wanted to sober up some before heading home.

All the doors were locked every night when I left. Who had a means and a motive for going in there only one night a week? There was a lump in my throat every winter Thursday morning! On some morning, would I find him there?

Shirley E. Juracek, Fairview School District 75,
Yankton County, SD, 1945-50

THE FIRST SCHOOL I taught in had an oil stove in the middle of the floor. The second one, with a basement, had a large coal furnace with a grate in the middle of the floor. One morning after I attempted to bank the furnace so as to have fire by morning, crayons melted and ran down towards the floor of one desk close to the grate. Each morning thereafter as I crested the hill, I would anxiously look to see if the school was still standing.

Ada May Geppert Foster, Beulah 2 and Lonetree 1,
Hanson County and Charles Mix County, SD, 1951-55

The Three Rs

IN 1929, AT AGE 16, I graduated from high school. That fall
I enrolled at Southern State Teachers College in Springfield. As I
remember, a year's tuition was $90, and even that was hard to
finance. Most of us were lucky to afford one year of college.
Fortunately, country schools were plentiful, and we were all able
to find jobs. After completing my year of training, I had to apply
for a permit to teach since I was only 17, and age 18 was required.
Fortunately, my grades were good, and the permit was issued.

My first day at school was quite a surprise. I had only
thirteen students–one in second grade, two in third, three in fourth,
two in fifth, two in sixth, two in seventh, and one in eighth.
My biggest surprise was that my 8th grader was a year older than

I and considerably larger. One seventh grader, a brother to the eighth grader, was the same age as I and also much larger.

In those years, farm work was considered by some parents to be more important than school–thus leaving the child to receive a hit-and-miss education. It was quite common to have a two-week "corn-picking vacation." Corn was hand-picked then, and the older children were quite adept at picking.

The following year, a large family moved into my district, and my student enrollment was up to nineteen. That year I had a charming little first grader who spoke no English. Her folks had come from Czechoslovakia and all she had ever learned was Czech. Since I neither spoke nor understood Czech, I had a few anxious moments! She was fortunately very intelligent, and with the cooperation of the rest of the students, who had been instructed to speak only English to her, she did quite well. Most of the other students did speak Czech, and once or twice in emergencies, they translated for me.

Our schoolhouse was heated by an old Round Oak stove. Water was brought in from a well in the yard. I had each pupil bring a cup or glass and we marked their names on them. They were told the dipper was to be used only to fill their cups, not to drink from.

Chores were assigned weekly, with the heavier chores–fuel and water hauling–going to the upper grades. Cleaning blackboards and sweeping were left for the lower grades. Everyone had some assigned chore.

We all brought our lunches, and we had fun games while we ate. We would start with the youngest. They would say "on my way to school I saw," and they would describe what they saw but not name it. The first one to guess correctly was next to tell what he or she saw–rabbit, cow, bird, etc. This game was enjoyed by all. They didn't realize it, but they were being taught to be observant and also how to express themselves.

I truly believe the country school offered much more than the "three Rs."

Louise Ranek, McCrea School,
Bon Homme County, SD, 1930-32

MY SCHOOL HAD DOUBLE DESKS, which because of their structure required seating everyone close together. The top of one desk served as work space for the students seated behind it, while the seats on the front served two students who sat in front of the desktop. Their desk had seats for the two pupils in front, and so on. One could not jiggle one's seat a bit closer or farther away from the desk top, since that would influence three other students. Typically in the morning we would push and pull to everyone's near-satisfaction, or until Miss Gramita stopped the arguing.

When everyone was seated, Miss Gramita would ask us to stand and recite the Pledge of Allegiance. The Pledge would be followed either by learning musical scales—do, re, mi, fa, so, la, ti, do—or fifteen minutes of singing from *The Golden Song Book*.

Another beginning activity was "current events" morning. The school subscribed to a small weekly news magazine, from which the teacher made assignments for oral reports. It was an excellent manner of learning public speaking.

As the older grades concentrated on their lessons, my sister would go to the recitation area at the front for her reading lesson. Miss Gramita hung a reading chart she had made from wrapping paper and pictures cut from various magazines. With a pointer moving to each word, she would read the sentences below a picture of a small girl—"I am a girl." Ruth would repeat the sentence as the pointer moved along. She would be corrected if the pronunciation was not acceptable. Then—"I am a little girl," and the first grader would read the line as the pointer led the little reader along. And so it went—"My hair is brown" . . . "I go to school." The teacher flipped the wrapping paper sheets from the "little girl" story to "little boy" to "See the dog" to "See the horse." Her fifteen-minute class over, Ruth and her classmate would return to their desks to read similar stories in a beginning reader. Or there would be some cutting and pasting to do, or paging through a story book, or perhaps just napping. Little ones were allowed to nap, but woe unto anyone in second grade who did that!

Arithmetic classes inevitably drew the attention of most students because they always included chalkboard exercises. The teacher gave the math problems, and each student would write on the board and do the computations, always with an effort not to show the answers to the student next to him/her. Always there was the "slow" one who had to be corrected by either the teacher or one of the better students. Flash cards were popular, since there was a spirit of competition.

A group of spelling words was assigned every week, and one method of learning was chalkboard practice. Generally on Fridays, there came the written test. What one missed was added to the next week's list.

Our Webster's Unabridged Dictionary was a favorite with its many animal and bird pictures and a double page of nations' flags. We were allowed to pull down the large maps mounted like window shades in a rack. We would find a flag and the nation's name and then find it on the map. We learned more geography through play than modern children do with far greater resources.

Friday's art classes were especially welcome. First, they signalled the coming weekend, and second, they caused considerable bustling about. Within a broad scope of learning activities, there was a modicum of freedom of movement and talking. The little ones would make elementary color wheels; the intermediate students made more sophisticated ones, and the sixth graders went as far as their imaginations sent them–making miniature horses, cows, cars, and tractors instead of the typical circles.

Some periods were spent on classical paintings. There we first learned of Michelangelo Buonarroti, Vermeer, and a dozen others. We learned perspective from pictures and then from drawing our own. Miss Gramita would point up shading, proportion, scale and view point, contrast and complementation. At year's end, each student's portfolio was carried home to the parents. The most promising work was displayed at the county-wide Young Citizens' League meeting in the spring.

Leo J. Neifer, Dewey School District,
McPherson County, SD, 1929-36

THE DEPRESSION OF THE THIRTIES promoted down-to-earth teaching challenges. Our one-teacher rural school had an enrollment of twenty-five pupils in all eight grades. We followed the prescribed South Dakota Course of Study, but needed something extra to strengthen our Sutley community. With the permission of the three-member school board, the teacher placed a workbench with a few practical woodworking tools at the disposal of boy pupils. Our enrollment had a majority of older boys. They had the energy to be troublemakers, but a major goal was to build a model farm.

Models are good, three-dimensional teaching devices used in construction and home-building, as well as in the television and movie-making industries. We wrote to the extension departments of land grant colleges in our neighboring states for information on building architectural models. We took a survey of the farm buildings in our community. We decided to build a modest farm house and a huge barn similar to the largest barn in our community.

Model making needs to be uniform, so we decided to build everything to a scale of one foot to one inch. The model house was completed first so the girl pupils could paint and decorate the walls and plan for the furniture and appliances. The community mothers became interested in the model and started to page through mail order catalogues for ideas that would be practical. The boys, likewise, when they had their measurements from home, determined the number of cow and horse stalls.

The boys studied the construction of the wagon, sleds, hay racks, header boxes and special haying equipment. Auxiliary sheds for poultry, swine, machinery and range cattle were added. They were all built to scale.

Our school then was in session only eight months. We did not complete the project the first year, but placed several completed buildings in the All School County Exhibit. The response stimulated the students to continue the models.

This project had the interest of the county superintendent of schools and the county extension agent. They supervised the formation of a Handcraft 4-H Club. We met monthly and did more practical woodworking projects for girls and boys. By the end of the third year, we took our model farm to the State Fair Exhibit in Huron.

Henry N. Stein, Buckenberger School,
Campbell County, SD, 1933-36

I WAS FORTUNATE to have a string of very good teachers in my eight years. Mom was on the school board and she fought to keep the more experienced and expensive teacher while other board members wanted a "summer school wonder" who would have accepted much less money. Mom fought fiercely one year to get $300 a month for our good teacher. She got it and I was glad because I loved Mrs. McCumber.

We were taught penmanship at least one period a week. We learned the Palmer method, which involved rolling the entire arm on the paper so one could get a nice, circular motion going and turn out nice, flowing letters. Mrs. McCumber practiced this method and her writing was always beautiful. I was always a problem because I was left-handed. She refused to let me write upside down as many lefties do, and eventually I adapted to the process. We made rows of h's and y's, turning them upside down to see if their symmetry matched. I loved these exercises, despite my left-handedness, but many kids, boys especially, hated them.

My favorite time of the whole week was art period on Friday afternoons. Mrs. McCumber explored all kinds of avenues with us. We tried watercolors, making things with coping saws, making silhouettes, etc. Once she found an alcohol-burning woodburner to be used in making woodburned pictures.

We took turns and all got a chance to make a picture with her one machine. My sister and I liked doing the pictures so well that Mom bought us a machine and we turned out lots of projects that winter.

Getting enough books to keep us avid readers busy was a problem. Our county Superintendent of Schools, Mr. DeBoer, would come around several times a year with books to share. How we looked forward to his visits! He always had some kind of science experiment to share with us. I can still remember how he would suck an egg into a milk bottle by creating a vacuum with a burning candle that took the air out of the bottle. We learned all kinds of principles of science. He always brought a box of several dozen books to lend us until the next time he came. I usually managed to check out all of them and read them. Once Mr. DeBoer brought Badger Clark, Poet Laureate of South Dakota, to the school. He read several of his poems to us and taught us how to write poetry. We were so impressed with that soft-spoken man with a beard. I practiced writing poetry for months, but never came up with anything very satisfactory.

Phylis Brunken, Law School,
Douglas County, SD, 1934-42

THE COUNTY SUPERINTENDENT visited school once a year, and that was usually in the fall. She would bring five or six books, and they were added to the library. Later on, we had a travelling library, that allowed us to exchange books with neighboring schools, and that way the students got to read more books.

Ruth Graves Ellis, McKay and Heaton Schools,
Charles Mix County, SD, 1940s

WE WOULD HAVE READING, arithmetic, spelling, writing, geography, history and science. Most of the work was done on the blackboard so the teacher could see if we were doing it right. Then at test time, the teacher would write the questions on the board, and we had to copy them on paper and write our answers. We had no homework unless we had been absent. Each class was about 10 minutes long, except music and art. Some of the classes were combined, like 3rd and 4th grades, 5th and 6th grades, and 7th and 8th grades. One year we did 3rd, 5th or 7th grade work, and the next year we did the 4th, 6th and 8th grade work. Subjects combined were science, health, history, geography and grammar. We were expected to get our work done while the teacher was holding another class.

For music, all the pupils sang the songs with the record on the phonograph or with the piano if the teacher could play.

Johanna Schutz, Burma School District 69,
Lincoln County, SD, 1930-35

OUR TOTAL STUDENT BODY WAS FIVE STUDENTS, I being the youngest. My sister was a year ahead of me. The other three were in the 7th and 8th grades. I remember being fascinated, listening to their discourse during the geography and history sessions. A significant feature about geography was that the large map of the United States was posted on the north wall of the school. North on the map was really north. The world globe was placed next to the map. This established a sense of direction for me that has lasted all my life. Every school should adopt that arrangement.

Donald E. Buss, Fiddle Creek School,
Fall River County, 1920-21

OUR SCHOOL WAS BI-CULTURAL. It was named after Native American Frank Owen. Three generations of his family attended the school. Our teacher taught all eight grades. She could handle it well, except for the slow learners or those who missed a lot of school. She would ask me to help them with arithmetic, reading and spelling. This was my start at setting my future, for I wanted to become a teacher in a one-room school just like mine.

I did teach school after graduating from high school in 1951. I went to ten weeks of summer school to get a certificate. This allowed me to teach in a rural school. I taught for three winters before raising my own family. My children went to a rural school until 1968, when it was closed and the bus hauled them to town.

Dorothy Althoff Pies, Owen School District #175,
Day County, SD, 1939-47

Prairie Patriots

WE MARCH AND WE SING; our voices ring; young citizens are we;
Leagued in a host whose watch-words are Youth, Courage, Loyalty.
Hailing our nation's banner, afloat in the sunlit sky,
Which through hopes and fears, through future years,
We will hold evermore on high.

Young Citizens' League March Song Chorus

TEACHERS AT SCHOOLS IN OUR REGION faced a particular language difficulty, for the students were all from German-speaking families. The little ones had very limited or no knowledge of English—except for a few "naughty words" picked up from older brothers. I remember well the rule against German being spoken anywhere on the school premises. Miss Gramita had a system whereby all the students, except first graders, were required to report all offenses once a week, typically as part of our Y.C.L. meetings.

The Young Citizens' League meeting was always a significant event, almost as valued as Friday art classes. Following Roberts Rules of Order, a slate of officers was nominated and elected. The president would assign duties: raising the flag, lowering the flag, carrying out ashes, filling the coal bucket, cleaning the chalkboard erasers—which amounted to pounding them against the outside of the school building, sweeping the floor, dusting the globe and window sills, passing out and collecting *The Golden Song Books* for morning singing. All were assigned work commensurate with our ages and abilities.

Leo J. Neifer, Dewey School District,
McPherson County, SD, 1929-36

I RECALL A Y.C.L. in the school district which taught many political and moral lessons and initiated spelling bees and other events. One enthusiastic teacher introduced moonlight parties for Y.C.L. families in our school. On the full moon night of the month, we all gathered at one home. Young and old played tag, hide and seek, and other games, and sometimes sang around a large outdoor campfire, if the home was small. Refreshments were provided by the host family; lemonade or hot cocoa and homemade cookies or doughnuts were devoured. Sometimes we skated on the river in the winter. Parental involvement was not a problem and we had fun.

Wilma Price, Milberg School, Butte County, SD, 1930s

ONE AFTERNOON I was visiting the Warn School and had been politely seated in a folding chair by the Y.C.L. hostess for the day. I was enjoying the lessons being presented when I began to feel myself sinking, and very slowly but surely the folding chair sank to the floor with me on it. Without a titter in the school, the teacher's chair was hastily pushed to the back of the room, and class resumed. Only one of the many interesting things I encountered in my 17 years as county superintendent.

Betty Larrington, Warn School,
Potte County, SD, 1956-70

OFTEN AT THE CLOSE OF OUR Y.C.L. meeting, our teacher, Lucia Parish (Qualm), would provide some entertainment. One particular day she wrapped penny candy bars with slips of paper and hid them. If you found one of these and carried out the skit written on your slip, you could keep the candy bar.

I found one, and oh how I wanted that candy! My slip said, "Sit with the prettiest girl in school." Slowly I sidled down the aisle and very carefully sat on the outside edge of a double desk seat of a little first grade girl. Whereupon she slid out the opposite side very quickly.

I got the candy bar and the girl. We recently celebrated our 50th wedding anniversary.

James A. Nachtigal, LaRoche School District 1,
Charles Mix County, SD, 1931

The Hickory Stick

LATE AFTERNOON SLANTED ACROSS THE STUBBLE FIELD, but Lizzie Kuehn, standing in the doorway of the shanty, was not looking at the grass turning green, eager as she was for spring to come to the Dakota prairie. She shaded her eyes. She thought she could make out two small figures in the distance. The new teacher must've given 'em problems, Easter coming on or not. She thought they did seem loaded down with books. Air was still nippy, all right. She shut the door, and the small house was dark. She was putting cobs into the stove when the two of them came in. She jerked around when she heard books being tossed into a corner.

"We quit school, Mamma. For good," Emmy said. Lizzie turned, but she just looked at them. "Frankie and me quit." Emmy's small chin quavered.

"How's that?" Lizzie asked.

"That mean ol' teacher!" Emmy said, angry tears brimming. "She made us stay after school. An' we up and quit!"

The whole story tumbled out then. The new teacher, Lily Wentworth, all of eighteen herself, had been writing something on the blackboard. One of the big boys in the back of the room shot a spitwad and hit the map right above her head. She turned around and saw Frank Kuehn with his hand raised. The teacher decided he must be the culprit, and she sentenced him to stay after school for an hour. "I said he didn't do it," Emmy choked, wiping her eyes. "An' she said, 'You can stay an hour, too!'" Just to think of it made Emmy cry, and she ran to her mother and threw her arms around her. "We ain't never goin' back to that 'ol school, Mamma."

"There, there now," Lizzie said, hugging the small girl. She gave her son a long, steady look.

"I didn't do it, Ma. I know who 'twas, but it warn't me," Frank said. "You want some more cobs?" She nodded. After he was gone, she washed Emmy's face and brushed her soft brown hair back from her warm temples.

At the table, where the four of them sat when Pa had unhitched the wagon and come in for supper, the children told again what had happened at school. They said they were never goin' back, it wasn't fair, and she couldn't do that to them. For a while, Frank Kuehn, Sr., sat without comment. He chewed his food slowly, wiped his dark mustache, then looked at his freckle-faced son. "You never throwed one of them spitballs?" he asked. "Never?"

"Well, sure. I've thrown 'em. Some. But it warn't me today."

"I know. I know it, Franky. But she didn't know, did she?"

The children looked at him and finally shook their heads. They saw the logic in what he said, but they still smarted under the humiliation of staying an hour for something they did not do. "It'll be a mite peculiar," Lizzie said, "when she comes to board 'n' room with us, an' you two not goin' to school any more."

"When's that?" the two of them asked.

"Next fall. When the new house is finished."

"You goin' to start the house, Pa? When? How soon?" Frank asked. He wanted to be a carpenter, and he was looking forward to pounding nails and sawing boards.

"Soon," Pa said. "Uncle Charlie's comin' up from Ioway to help."

"Kin I help you, too?" Frank asked.

"An' me?"

Pa smiled at them both and nodded. "You both can," he said, "just as soon's school's out." They looked at him, but they did not protest. They could see he had something more on his mind. "This's a mighty big country. It's goin' to take big men and women to run it. Them that's got the learnin's got the edge. That right, Ma?"

She smiled at him. "Yes," she said. "Why children, 'fore most of the folks round here got houses built for themselves, the men folk went down to Pearl Creek an' built that one-room school. Pa helped fore you two was even big enough to go."

Jeannette Kinyon, based on her father's experience,
Pearl Creek Area School, c. 1894

46

IN 1924, WHEN I WAS SEVEN YEARS OLD, I attended school with eight other students, one being a sister five years older than I. I was the youngest child in our school and in first or second grade. All students in our school were Lakota Indians.

Our teacher was Miss Hines, and I remember her very clearly. She was a blue-eyed blonde. I was the youngest child in my family and came from a Lakota-speaking home. English was not a language I understood. Miss Hines was not a Lakota speaker. I remember she would stand there and point her finger at me and would seem very upset at me, and I could not understand why. She had a set of flash cards that had the upper case letters of the alphabet on them, and she would sit with me since I was the only student in my grade, and I was to tell her what letter she was showing me. To me the letters R and B looked the same, and she seemed very frustrated with me because I kept confusing them. To me everything about school and the English language was confusing and frustrating.

To make matters worse, I was learning to write my name. My name, Ollie Not Stampede, was very long. We had a large map on the wall, and I remember one day when I was totally frustrated about writing my name, I looked at that map and saw the word *Asia* written on it. It was then that I decided I liked that name for my last name. It was short and easy to write. We were to fold our papers in half lengthwise and write our names on the top. I very nicely finished my paper and wrote "Ollie Asia" on it. I couldn't understand why Miss Hines got so upset. She told me that was not my name, and I was to go to the chalkboard and write my first and last name. The next time I was to write my name on an assignment, I wrote "Ollie Asia." I spent a lot of time at the chalkboard, writing "Ollie Not Stampede" over and over again.

Ollie Napesni, Todd County Public School, SD, 1924

47

ONE DAY WHEN I WAS IN SECOND GRADE, the student two seats ahead of me needed help from the teacher. Miss Mortimer was quite tall, and her skirt hemline was just below the knee. When she bent over to help the student at the small desk, her hemline at the back rose just a little higher. Ardel, who sat just ahead of me, found that hemline was just below his eye level. He couldn't resist the desire to lean over and observe what the well-dressed schoolteacher looked like under her skirt. His head brushed her skirt in the process, and Miss Mortimer had Ardel in tow in nothing flat. She dragged him past her desk, where she picked up a triangle wood ruler and then dragged him outside. Thus she spared the rest of the school the trauma of watching her beat the h___ out of Ardel. Today, if a teacher whipped a student, she would be in trouble with the parents. Miss Mortimer boarded at Ardel's home. When his mother heard of what Miss Mortimer had done, she did the same thing. Just a few years ago, Ardel and I discussed the good old days, and he said, "Even if I knew I would get a whipping, I would do it again!"

Tom Shonley, Long School, Aurora County, SD, 1931-35

THERE WERE NO DISCIPLINE PROBLEMS because if you misbehaved up in school, you got paddled upon arrival at home. You were at school to learn.

Fred A Beeman, Cottonwood School District #68,
Tripp County, SD

ONE AFTERNOON when we were on the way home, we came to the road where two of my students, the Picek boys, turned off. The boys took out cigarettes and lit them. They said, "Ha, ha, you can't do anything to us now, since we are on our own property."

Evelyn Myers Sharping, Olson School,
Brule County, SD, 1947

H o t P o t a t o e s

EVERYONE CARRIED A LUNCH PAIL IN THOSE DAYS. It was usually a syrup pail with a metal lid that was difficult to pry off, or a lard pail—those were easier to open. Lunch buckets were usually set out in the coatroom, except in extremely cold weather, when we could bring them inside. Once in a while the kids and the teacher enjoyed hot meals together in the colder months. What a treat! Some moms would send potatoes along with their youngsters, and the teacher would put them atop the huge, round heating stove. Coal was the fuel, and the teacher was the early-bird janitor who poked the banked fire alive in the morning and got the schoolroom warm. Well, those potatoes were heavenly, having baked all

50

forenoon! I don't recall what we had to put on them. No doubt, butter, salt and pepper. We must have had some sort of small plate, and a knife and fork too.

Sometimes a mother would cook up a huge kettle of soup and the dad would take the soup along with the kids to school in the morning. The soup would be set atop the furnace. Now that was super!

Myra Dubbe Kalb, District 71 School,
Minnehaha County, 1921-26

I ATTENDED COUNTRY SCHOOL IN TRIPP COUNTY in the 1920s. In those days we had several commodities from the government, but the only one I remember is powdered milk. What a treat when our teacher used it to make hot cocoa to supplement the hearty lunches we brought from home!

Are you picturing the easily dissolved little granules we buy in the store today? Well, in 1925 it was as different from that as the slightly later but early-day margarine was from the Blue Bonnet of today. In case you don't remember, we had to break a little capsule of yellow coloring into a pound packet of something resembling lard and work it in, to have colored margarine.

The powdered milk was in chunks and pieces which had to be broken up to be dissolved, and even then it wasn't very smooth. But by adding some cocoa and sugar, our teacher made a drink that we seven students loved.

But I'm sure there must be some scientific reason why that drink was always hotter than boiling. Perhaps it was the air pressure, or the altitude, or even some chemical that also made the powdered milk lumpy. Or maybe it was just our tin cups. To this day, when I drink hot chocolate, I can feel the blistered lips and tongue I invariably had when we drank cocoa at school.

Frances Blessing Wagner, Irwin Township
School District 23, Tripp County, SD, 1923-30

THE CHILDREN I TAUGHT would sit in their own seats and eat their lunches. Times were hard, and the children from one family in particular brought very little to eat in their lunches. I discovered that all these children had to eat at noon was a sandwich made of poor bread with only lard and pepper between the two slices. When the area superintendent came by one day, I reported to him how little this family had to eat. I later learned that the Red Cross had helped them out with food deliveries.

Gladys Brewick, Sanborn County, SD, 1930s

IN THE WINTERTIME we did have hot lunches in school, after a fashion. The students took turns bringing something to serve hot to the whole school: hot cocoa, canned pork and beans, corn, peas or potatoes to bake in the coals of the furnace. I do not recall having homemade hot soups, but one teacher used the canned pork and beans (like today's Van Camps) to make soup. She just added water, and that was not very tasty! Once in a while when a family had butchered a beef, they would bring roast beef, mashed potatoes and gravy for everyone. What a treat! My mother did this, as did some others. Someone even brought homemade ice cream once, but that was disappointing, as the freezer leaked, and the salt mixture got into the ice cream. It was an old-fashioned hand-turned freezer.

Ida DeNeui Poppenga, Ashlawn School District #89,
Turner County, 1925-33

WE HAD A VERSION OF SCHOOL LUNCHES during the depression years. Commodities were given out by the county once a month. Our teacher obtained flour, dried milk, salt pork, raisins and peanut butter. She would ask each student to bring a large potato to school. One would bring an onion for flavor. She would put them into the hot ashes at the bottom of the furnace in the winter so they could bake. Then at noon she fried the salt pork to make a gravy for the potatoes. With seasonings, the crispy pieces were very good over the potato. The teacher would be tending to lessons and dinner at the same time. None of us complained about the lack of variety. Some had about the same food at home and accepted what they were given, as they had been served some bread and milk meals at home more than once.

Phylis Brunken, Law School,
Douglas County, SD, 1934-42

OUR SCHOOL WAS CLOSE TO A RAILROAD CROSSING. The hobos would get off the trains, walk to the schoolhouse, knock on the door, and scare us plenty. The teacher would ask if we had extra items to share. Of course, we'd dash to the syrup pail buckets to share homemade bread, or cookies, or a cupcake. Fruit was usually scarce, so it was not given up.

Joyce Michels Wittenhagen, Rose School,
Faulk County, SD, 1938

IN THE LATE FALL our lunch consisted of two slices of homemade bread with fresh rendered goose lard. We had "snow capped" lard (from a box Dad bought at the store) much of the rest of the year. During the winter months when the coal heater was keeping us warm, we would bring potatoes to school. We'd bury them in the ash pan and when dinnertime came, they were done!

During the war years (1939-45), we got rationed food for schools. It consisted mostly of cans of beans. Oh, was that ever a treat to heat them up on top of the coal heater. I always hoped I would get the piece of fat!

Dorothy Althoff Pies, Owen District School 175,
Day County, SD, 1939-47

WE BROUGHT OUR LUNCHES TO SCHOOL EACH DAY. The lunches were usually peanut butter and jelly sandwiches, pickles, raw carrots, apples, or plums. Some days we were lucky and had a cookie or a piece of cake. One day we brought a syrup pail of potato soup for our family. We put the pail on top of the stove to get warm before lunch time. We were all busy doing our penmanship, when all of a sudden, the top blew off the pail, and the potato soup flew to the ceiling and all over. What a mess, but I think it was the best potato soup I ever had. Next time the teacher was sure to open the lid before anything was set on top of the stove.

Johanna Schutz, Burma School District 69,
Lincoln County, SD, 1930-35

ONE OF MY EARLIEST MEMORIES OF SCHOOL is of milk break. The milkman brought individual bottles which were stored in the refrigerator in the basement, and we students anxiously awaited afternoon break when we could have our milk. One day we had a special treat—chocolate milk. Mine tasted terrible, but I was too shy to complain. So I just drank it. When I had finished, I brought the empty bottle to my teacher and said, "This didn't taste very good." She smelled the bottle and said, "My goodness, this milk was very sour!"

Janet Hovey Johnson, Sterling School District 42,
Brookings County, SD, 1960-65

Fun and Games

"SIX, SEVEN, EIGHT, NINE, TEN," the little voice shouted. "Ready or not, here I come." And the other six students at our country school held their collective breaths in the limited hiding places available in the fenced-in yard—actually a small corner of land out of my father's grain field.

But I, about ten years old, was experiencing more than the excitement of hide-'n-seek. I was being gently touched by the gallantry of young love.

In the northeast corner of the schoolyard, inside a small mountain of thistles, we children had hollowed out a tiny room, large enough for two little people to occupy.

To this hideout I had rushed, rather than going behind or inside the barn, between the two indoor toilets, inside the coal shed at the back of the schoolhouse, or in any of the corners made where that coal shed or the entry hall to the school itself was attached. The thistle room was by far the choice spot to hide, but so uncomfortable!

As I knelt down to enter, I found it already occupied by Edgar, who motioned me to keep coming. As I crawled in, he took off his jacket and spread it beside him in the only space available to me. As I squirmed my way in and settled next to him, with his jacket warm under me, he put his arm around me. I was overwhelmed! It was so unlike him! The boy with whom I pushed and ran and rough-housed during recess and lunch hour, every school day, was actually treating me like a girl! It was the beginning of a new me.

Frances Blessing Wagner, Tripp County, SD, 1923-30

ABOUT MIDDAY, THERE WAS A RECESS FOR ALL PUPILS. Those who liked sports and active games, especially baseball supervised by the teacher, could play. Any kid worth his salt learned to throw, catch and bat respectably.

The early baseball games were played with stuffed stockings for balls. There were no sport stores in those days, and bats were carved from old wagon tongues.

When someone's dad brought a real baseball from out of town, it was patched and sewn reverently until the cover fell off from age. Then the bare strings were taped with black electrician's tape over and over again, and it sailed an incredible distance when it was struck.

When some boy inherited a real baseball bat, it was cherished like King Arthur's scepter. Whoever broke it, by forgetting to hold the label up, was sent home with the broken pieces and the dire warning, "Your old man is gonna pay for this."

Mary Magirl Dougherty, Central School,
Tripp County, SD, 1922-23

SURPRISING AS IT MAY SEEM TODAY, some few would do school work during recess, usually the older ones who felt a scholastic threat hanging over them.

Leo J. Neifer, Dewey School District,
McPherson County, SD, 1929-36

WE HAD ROLLICKING RECESSES. Since we had all eight grades and twenty-five students, we had many games going at the same time. But we played softball much of the time with sides chosen from biggest to smallest kids, and all of us playing. The teacher always supervised, so we had few accidents and she tolerated no fighting. I have wondered when she got all her papers written and corrected. No wonder she didn't have time to find a boyfriend and get married for ten years.

Pat Speelman, Wayne #3 School,
Hanson County, SD, 1940s

SCHOOL PLAYGROUND EQUIPMENT WAS VERY SCARCE. One dad played baseball on the local team, and he sent out-of-use mitts and balls for us kids, and even bats, which took quite some muscle to swing—especially for the littler kids.

"Ante-I-over" was another game. We chose sides and threw the ball over the schoolhouse, and we'd catch it, run around to the opposite side, and "catch" as many as we touched with the ball.

When we girls were nearly teens, one who was about dating age taught us younger ones how to dance—two step, fox trot, waltz—and we'd do that at noon hour behind the school. That lasted but a short time because the lady who lived close to the school saw us and reported that we were dancing! So somebody had to do something about it! So we stopped that noontime diversion.

That woman and her husband AND their kids all eventually danced. What was so immoral about us 6th, 7th and 8th graders dancing?

Myra Dubbe Kalb, District 71 School,
Minnehaha County, SD, 1921-28

A FAVORITE PASTIME AT RECESS was what I call "chase." The boys chasing the girls and trying to catch them, maybe planting a kiss. The girls would flee to safety by running into the toilet en masse (sometimes 4 to 6 at a time) and locking the door and staying in there until one couldn't stand the smell any more. Much laughter, many secrets and gossip were shared in those small confines.

Marilyn Owen, Sunflower School District 112,
Saline County, NE, 1934-41

ON VERY COLD DAYS we were allowed to stay in the schoolhouse at noon and recess times. One of the things the girls did was to play jacks on the floor. I don't know what the boys did. Probably got into trouble. When weather permitted, we were outside building snow forts, playing Fox and Geese, and sometimes getting into not-always-friendly snowball fights which could result in a quick end of the recess or noon hour.

In warmer weather there was a mad dash to see who got the teeter-totter or giant stride. The giant stride was a tall metal pole with chains that hung down the sides. Each chain had two metal bars spaced about a foot apart on the bottom end. You grasped the metal bars and ran until you had enough speed to lift your feet off the ground, and for a few minutes, were able to swing free.

Gertrude Johnson, Howard School District 140,
Minnehaha County, SD, 1936-40

POM-POM-PULL-AWAY, tag, prisoners' base, kittenball (softball), merry-go-round playing, and ice skating were fun for our dozen or so kids in Florence #2 Country School. With spring breezes, we were especially attracted to the large pond only a few hundred feet away from the school.

During the noon hour in the spring, we would sometimes go to the pond, clamp our ice skates onto our shoes using a special key, and have fun skating. The pond was frozen solid from the cold of winter, but with the advance of spring, the pond would get a bit soft on the surface and the ice would get thinner, creating a rubbery surface that flexed downward with the weight of young skaters. This thinning process advanced from the edge of the pond toward the center.

One bright and warm spring day, we had a memorable experience in active learning. Those of us skating at the noon hour were supported by the rubbery and flexing ice as we made our way to the more solid ice at the center of the pond. But half an hour later when the school bell rang to call us back, there had been enough melting that we broke through the rubbery ice closer to the edge as we made our way back to school. We were soaked! For most of the afternoon, we dried out by sitting around the square floor grating above the basement furnace.

Duane E. Johnson, Florence School District 2,
Hamlin County, SD, 1939

OUR PLAYGROUND HELD MANY SPECIAL MEMORIES. In the snow we made a big pie shape for the tag games of "Fox and Goose" or "Cut the Pie." When the dam was frozen over, our young teacher would let us go play on it, not knowing that we couldn't hear when she rang the bell. In good weather our porch was base for the game of "Run Sheep Run."

We also played basic games of football and baseball. Those needed a number of players to make a game, so the older kids had to let the younger ones make up the team. Since our school attendance went from twelve, nine, seven and then to five students, games were not much fun unless we all joined in.

Our playground had very tall swings which were great once you got a good start. Our short legs didn't get us pumped high very fast, so we would beg the older kids to give us strong pushes. They usually didn't want to be bothered.

Janet Fairchild Snow, Elbon School,
Haakon County, SD, 1944-49

ON BAD DAYS WE PLAYED HIDE THE THIMBLE or games at the blackboard such as Cat and Hangman (when you guess the letter to make a word). With our Y.C.L. money we bought a Carrom board. We also purchased a Monopoly set. The game took so long that we would just leave it all set up and continue from where we had left off at the last recess.

Evelyn Myers Sharping, Swanson School,
Brule County, SD, 1931-39

Frank Douglas's children at Putney school, 1889. Ina, Tina, Nina, Ray and Rue. (Not pictured: Zena and Roy) Photo Courtesy of Dacotah Prairie Museum, Aberdeen, SD. Donated by Mary Alice Jensen.

Taught to the tune of a hickory stick. Manly, Iowa, June 26, 1897. South Dakota Historical Society.

Independent School #2, March 18, 1898. Edith Bridgman, teacher.
Photo courtesy of South Dakota State Historical Society, Pierre, SD.

Deadman Valley School–District 28, Stanley County.
Photo courtesy Karl Fischer, Ft. Pierre, SD and the
South Dakota State Historical Society, Pierre, SD.

*One room rural school. Location unknown. Photo Courtesy of Dacotah Prairie
Museum, Aberdeen, SD. Donated by Vera Kohlhoff.*

*Early day rural school. Location unknown. Photo Courtesy of Dacotah Prairie
Museum, Aberdeen, SD. Donated by Vera Kohlhoff.*

A South Dakota school with pot-bellied stove in 1902
South Dakota State Historical Society.

This is the way youngsters travelled to school during the homesteading era on the western Southe Dakota prairies. It took only seven horses to carry these 12 pupils to school in about 1912. South Dakota State Historical Society

Tripp County 1923. Mary Magirl Dougherty, the teacher standing far right, posed for this photograph with her class at the Central School Picnic, Tripp County, South Dakota in 1923. Roy Davis used a box camera to take this picture. Donated by Mary Dougherty Johnson.

An attentive class at North Bramhall School, Hand County, 1929. South Dakota State Historical Society.

Cane Creek School where Lily P. Hanson Kruse taught in 1935-36.

Boys playing football at Eggers School District 139, 1938.
Photo courtesy of Doris Eggers Huseboe.

Girls playing football at Eggers School District 139, 1938.
Photo courtesy of Doris Eggers Huseboe.

On the steps of McKinley School District 38, Yankton County, 1941-42. Left to right; back row, Lloyd Kuchta, Linda Klasi, Helen Medeck Kremer (the teacher), Dick Klasi, Bonnie King, Dorthy Kuchta and Mary Ann Fejfar. Front row, Keith Burns, James Fejfar and Eugene Barkley. Photo courtsey of Helen Medeck Kremer.

Birthday party at McKinley School District 38, Yankton County, 1956.
Left to right, back row: Danny Bierle and Mrs. Plown, the teacher. Front row:
Gail Kremer (Herman), Mar Kay Bierle, Donna Voil and Sharon Kremer Eggers.

Beginning the 1958-59 year at McKinly School District 38, Yankton, SD.
Photo courtesy of Sharon Eggers, Wakonda, SD.

Visiting the Eggers School District 139, built in 1909, one mile east and a mile north of the Renner Corner and moved to the Augustana College Campus, Sioux Falls in 1993. From left: Mary Gederos, Dorothy Robbins, Ken Robbins, Norma Wilson, Doris Eggers Huseboe (who attended the school for eight years and shared her experience), Charles Woodard and Michael Haug. Photo courtesy of Art Huseboe.

*Interior of the Eggers School, at Augustana College, Sioux Falls. From left:
Norma Wilson, Charles Woodard, Dorothy Robbins, Kenneth Robbins,
Michael Haug, Wayne Knutson, Mary Gederos and Doris Huseboe sharing
information about the school she attended for eight years.
Photo courtesy of Art Huseboe.*

*Interior of the one-room school operated by the Keystone Historic Museum,
Keystone, South Dakota, as a living history museum. Elementary schoolteachers
are invited to bring their classes to study in this environment each spring.
Photo courtesy of Herbert W. Blakey.*

Students, their parents and teachers playing balloon volleyball on the last day of school, May 6, 1998 at Como School, in Hand County. Photo courtesy of Sandy Sivertsen.

Sandy Sivertsen and her class at Como School: Left to right; back row, Pat Hasart, aide, Kyle Werdel, Kimi Werdel, Sandy Sivertsen and Lana Werdel. On left teeter totter, back to front; Courtney Knippling, Ward Kippling, and Shanna Sivertsen. On right teeter-totter, back to front: Jacob Knippling. Jake Waring and Emily Kippling. Photo courtesy of Sandy Sivertsen.

*Editors Charles Woodard and Norma Wilson doing research for this book at the
Eggers Schoolhouse on the Augustana College Campus, Sioux Falls, South Dakota,
June 1998. Dr. Woodard is a Professor of English at South Dakota State University
in Brookings; Dr. Wilson is a Professor of English at University of South Dakota.
Both received Ph.D.s in American Literature with an emphasis in American
Indian Literatures from the University of Oklahoma.*

RECESS WAS ONE OF THE BEST PARTS OF THE DAY. Each morning and afternoon we were given a 15-minute break. At noon we were able to play outside for another 30-45 minutes. Unsupervised play consisted of softball, running games, climbing rock piles, and in the winter, sledding down to the creek. Sledding was enhanced by a ramp made by the older boys from the school's window shutters. This sledding ramp started its route at the top of the hill at the end of the softball field. Invariably one person would go through the ice in the springtime. We were given the freedom and responsibility to look after ourselves and each other.

During the winter we often played grocery store at recess time. We all collected empty food containers from our homes and brought them to be set up throughout the schoolroom. One lucky person was chosen to be the store clerk. Others were shoppers. We learned as we played.

Jan Bertsch Quenzer, Detmold School District 2,
McPherson County, SD, mid-1950s–early 60s

THE BIG DAY HAD FINALLY ARRIVED! Pleasant View School was taking on the Jones West Central School in a game of football. This was the big grudge match of '68. Sure, they had whipped us in a girly game of softball, but in a real man's game of football, we were gonna annihilate them. We had been preparing for several weeks, and had even written up and numbered a few secret "plays" that were sure to devastate their unorganized defenses. Although none of us had pads, most of us had dredged up a helmet from an older brother or from an old box of toys. We looked fairly sharp in our uniforms—work shoes, blue jeans and white t-shirts.

As we piled out of our teacher's car, our opponents spilled out of their schoolhouse door. They looked ill-prepared—no uniforms, no helmets, not even a playbook. Furthermore, some of them were girls! No matter; the girls would have to suffer the consequences just like the rest.

Since we were the visiting team, we had the privilege of receiving the first kickoff. The kick was surprisingly deep; I had to scramble backwards to get it. Before I had time to move forward and demonstrate my blazing gridiron speed, I was hit with bone-crunching impact—by a girl! It was unbelievable. One of the Stevicks girls had tackled me harder than I had ever been tackled.

"All right," I thought to myself, "if those guys want to play rough, we'll give them rough!" From the huddle I called our best play. "Old number one," I said. "And don't have any mercy on them girls—they hit pretty hard."

I lined up behind our three-man line and took the snap from our big man in the middle, Kevin Miner. Our deadly wedge was sure to push right through their scrawny defenses. Soon they'd be sorry they had ever accepted this challenge.

"Ready... set... hike!" The ball felt good between my hands as I prepared to move forward behind our advancing wedge. I could see the goal line only 30 yards or so ahead, marked by the edge of the girls' toilet.

WHAM, WHAM... I was knocked roughly backwards to the ground. Agitated, I lifted my helmet out of my eyes to see who could have possibly penetrated our iron-clad offensive line. More than likely it was that Hanson kid or Johnny Vosika, who was built pretty good and fast too. "Oh, no," I groaned to myself, "it was those dang Stevicks girls again!"

Okay, so pure brawn didn't work. Then we'd have to use brains and sophistication. Who did they think they were messing with, anyway? I called play #2 and gave the handoff to Kerner. Roger wasn't that fast, but once he got moving, he was hard to stop. The handoff was downright sneaky, well-executed too, and sure to fool them for a second or two. WHAM...WHAM! Roger moaned as we helped him to his feet. He didn't say anything, just glared at the Stevicks girls as he limped back to the huddle.

"All right, who wants to take the ball this time?" I glanced around the small circle, but everyone's eyes stayed glued to the ground. Since there were no immediate volunteers, I asked my brother, "How about you, Marly, you wanna blast one around the end?" Marly was the fastest guy on our team and was certain to find a chink in their defenses. He licked his bruised lips nervously and rubbed a sore shoulder. Apparently the line was taking a beating also.

"Sure," he nodded reluctantly, "I'll give her a try." He didn't sound nearly as confident now as he had on the trip over. On the way back to the line, Kerner whispered in his ear, "Stay away from those Stevicks girls, Braun, it hurts when they hit you."

Our line dug in, Marly one step behind us, a determined look on his face. He took the snap and headed around the left end. I pulled back to run interference for him, and things were looking real good too, until that Hanson kid took me out. I saw the ball fly out of Marly's hands as the youngest of the Stevicks girls knocked him flat. The older one scooped up the fumble and ran it in for a touchdown.

They beat us 45 to 7 that day. On the trip home as we nursed our injuries, we discussed how to regain our lost honor. Our decision was unanimous. When we met the Stevicks girls again, it would not be on the playing field, but at the rink for a friendly session of roller skating.

Marvin Braun, Pleasant View School,
Gregory County, SD, 1968

Mean Streaks

THERE WAS ANOTHER SIDE. Gangs were also in style many long years ago. Some of the boys were experts at swearing. I had never been around anyone who had such filthy language before, and I was sworn at for nothing but being in their vision. It cut me to the core. I quickly learned how to keep out of the way of certain individuals who could be so gross. It must not have entered our teacher's mind that very gross things were happening on the playground. She did lecture us for an hour once on our behavior—but actions speak louder than words. It was a big relief when the older bullies graduated and we could enjoy school again!

Anonymous

OFTEN OUR NAMES WERE A REASON FOR TEASING. A slow-learning kid's name would become a synonym for stupidity. So anyone pulling something stupid would be called that name. My husband tells of a Dutch immigrant girl coming to school. Her first name was "Shitska." When her parents discovered the bad connotations of the name in English, they changed her name to "Helen." Kids could be very cruel. Boys made fun of girls and girls made fun of boys. Any weakness became something to provoke names such as "Zitface" or "Fatty." Somehow we survived, and most of us grew up to be productive adults.

Phylis Brunken, Douglas County, SD, 1934-42

MY YOUNGER BROTHER always wanted to go to school with me, but he wasn't old enough. We lived only a quarter mile from the school, so at recess time, he'd run away from home, and come to school.

Boys, teenagers, delighted in taking him out to the horse barn. They'd tease him, getting up on top of the rafters, until he lost his temper and cried. He'd pick up dried, powdery horse manure to throw at them. Of course, it fell back on top of him, mixed with tears and saliva, a MESS!

One winter day, one of the 16-year-old boys decided he wanted to leave school right after lunch. The teacher said, "No!" He picked up a big block of wood and held it over his head, threatening to hit her with it if she didn't let him out the door. I was seven years old and loved the teacher. I stood in front of her to protect her. The result was that he didn't hit her, but she was afraid I'd get hurt, so she let him go. He was later expelled from school for a few days, which was what he wanted in the first place.

Rozella Bracewell, Riggs School,
Meade County, SD, 1927-34

OUR RECESS TIME was unsupervised and sometimes we got into mischief. One time the older boys and girls pushed an unpopular teacher's car into the ditch. One of the girls got worried about the possible consequences of their actions, and she walked about a quarter of a mile home, hitched up a team of mules, came back and pulled it out—all before the teacher knew about it, or maybe she chose not to know.

Marilyn Owen, Sunflower School District 112,
Saline County, NE, 1936

THE KIDS MADE IT AWFUL ROUGH for one especially strict teacher. I've always remembered one prank we played on her. No wonder she lasted only one year! One winter school day, out in the school yard, we hatched a plan to get even with this "mean" teacher. That winter there was a lot of snow, with snowbanks that covered the trees of the Bishop Tree Claim next to the schoolhouse. Only the tops of the trees stuck out of the snowbanks. We spent our recesses that winter digging tunnels in the snow and our plans for the teacher slowly developed from that. We dug a deep, deep pit in a snowbank and then laid lathe across the top if it. Carefully, we covered it with snow so you couldn't even see the big hole. Little did the teacher know what was in store for her, as we talked her into coming outside to play! We asked her to play "follow the leader." The "leaders," of course, knew exactly where the pit was dug and jumped over it, but the poor teacher didn't know, and down she dropped! You couldn't even see her after she fell in the hole in the snowbank. We had to get a ladder for her to get out of the snow pit. While we all thought this was very funny, our teacher thought otherwise. We all lost a lot of recesses for this prank!

Delbert Rawden, Chambers School,
Faulk County, SD, 1925-30

WE LIVED A MILE FROM THE SCHOOLHOUSE and Highway 42 was then newly-gravelled. One day, after the school day was over, a neighbor girl and I started toward home just behind the girl's oldest brother. He picked up a stone from the new gravel, turned around and aimed it at my face. He hit my nose, and I went screaming back to the schoolhouse. The teacher comforted me and wiped the blood from my face and walked home with me.

This bully never apologized, and neither did his dad. The folks didn't take me to a doctor, so the upshot of that experience was that my nose grew crooked inside. The septum is curved so that one side gets all stuffed up easily when I have a cold. Otherwise, it looks normal.

Three years ago this bully and his wife visited me. I said—in front of his wife—that I still remembered him breaking my nose. He flinched and said, "Oh! I thought you had forgotten that!"

It sure shocked his wife.

The fellow died two years ago, about a year after I told him I remembered.

Forget? Hah!

Myra Kalb, District 21 School, Minnehaha County, SD, 1921

WHITES ARE PREJUDICED AT TIMES against Native Americans, but it also works the other way around. One family's last name was French; both parents looked Native American. Their son had blonde curly hair. The other students would call him "White Bread." He had a super attitude and would yell back, "Crust."

Sandy Sivertsen, Wanblee School,
Kadoka District, 1989-90

The Human Comedy

ONCE WHEN I WENT TO SIGN A CONTRACT for the school year, the school director, after questioning my ability as a teacher, sitting across from me, chewing tobacco, gave one long aim with his cud, landing it in a mouse hole in the center of the room. Then he said, "One thing I want you to do in the school is to teach them manners!"

Mary Magirl Dougherty, Schoolhouse School, 1918

ONE DAY OUR TEACHER, who was a good-sized lady, leaned back too far on her swivel chair, flipping over backwards. Most of the students laughed, but I was worried about her safety. Well, the only thing she hurt was her dignity, and she was always grateful to me for rushing to help her out of her predicament.

Eileen Iverson, West Point School, Clay County, SD, 1935

ONE SPRING MORNING when the gophers had appeared after a long winter, three of the younger boys decided to catch some of them by pouring water into their hole. As the gophers came out of the hole, they caught them and put them in a paper box and closed it. They poked a few small holes in the side of the box for air. The gophers were wet, so they brought them into the schoolhouse and asked the teacher whether they could set the box with the gophers next to the stove. The teacher allowed it. After a while, the gophers warmed up and dried. They soon started looking for a way to escape. All of a sudden the gophers were running around in the schoolhouse. The teacher climbed on her chair and screamed, "Open the door and let them out!" There was quite a commotion until the gophers ran out the door. The teacher made it clear to everyone not to let this type of thing happen again.

Ervin Schumacher, Long Lake School District 2,
McPherson County, SD, 1938

WHEN YOU TAUGHT IN A COUNTRY SCHOOL, you walked to school from your boarding place. Sometimes the air was humid, and most times the walks were exhilarating, but often in the winter season it was very cold, so I wore two-piece snowsuits. I arrived at school one morning and discovered I had neglected to put on a skirt before I stepped into the snowpants. So I had to keep the pants on all day. Three of my pupils accepted my dilemma well, but the fourth pupil, the seventh grade boy, kept giggling. He giggled and giggled to the point where it was disruptive, so I hesitantly sent him home. There his parents put him to work for his misbehavior. He was sent out to clean the barns. Years later, we both enjoyed a good chuckle over that incident.

Astrid Raad, District 67 School,
Brookings County, SD, 1941-42

I SPENT EIGHT YEARS in a one-room school house at Academy and that same school is still in use today.

About all I can remember about the first grade is that when the two of us first graders had to recite, we had to sit in the seat on the front row of desks. One day the teacher asked us to name insects.

"Grasshoppers," I said.

"Flies," said another first grader.

"Ants," I said.

"Pissants," said the other first grader. Somehow I knew that wasn't the right answer.

Ralph Nachtigal, LaRoche School District 1,
Charles Mix County, SD, 1938

EXCEPT FOR ONE FAMILY, all the children I taught lived within walking distance, and they'd quite frequently stop in at the cottage where I lived. They loved to walk me to school. One beautiful September morning, I noticed Noble, my first grader, and his cousin Don, who was in the third grade, coming. They were all smiles and in deep conversation. Don was carrying something on his head. When I saw it was a pie that wasn't wrapped—not even in a newspaper, I was puzzled.

Don gave the pie to me and said, "Mom made this for you." He then warned me not to let his sister Verla see it in case she stopped by. I thanked him and said I'd put it away so Verla wouldn't see it. Verla did stop by, with an invitation from her mother to come to their house for supper that evening. I didn't mention the pie.

The first thing I noticed as we stepped into the kitchen was the long table all set and a kerosene lamp on each end. After an introduction to their mother, Mabel, whom as yet I hadn't met, she busied herself dishing up the food which would soon satisfy some hungry appetites. Mr. Veal, the father, did the seating. I was right opposite Don. Everything went well. Lots of good food and conversation until it came time for dessert.

Then Mabel excused herself from the table and went to the southwest corner of the room where stood a large, white cupboard. After a short while she asked Verla to come over there. I heard her say in an undertone, "Where is the other pie?" Don kept shoveling in food. At the same time he gave me a pleading look, as much as to say, "What shall we do?"

I felt like I had to come to the rescue, so I said, "I wouldn't care for any pie." After a bit Don said he wouldn't care for any either.

It didn't take Mr. Veal long to figure things out. He looked at me and then at Don and burst out laughing. He knew where the pie was. That hearty laugh made me know that everything would be all right. I took the pie to school the next day, and we all had a sample of it and enjoyed it to the last crumb.

Emma Sittner Nelson, Chance School,
Perkins County, SD, 1939

LITTLE DONNY WAS ONE OF MY FIRST GRADERS. He was a sweet-faced, white-haired boy whose complexion and strong Danish dialect revealed his ancestry. Donny lived on the highway I travelled every day back and forth to school. His dad drove him to school each morning, but couldn't take off from his farming work in mid-afternoon to bring him home, and he didn't want him walking home on the busy, narrow highway.

Since I passed that way on my trip home, he asked if I would be willing to drop Donny off. I agreed and found it to be profitable, since each Friday he had me back up to his gas tank and fill my car.

One day in early spring, the kids had been particularly restless. My patience had been stretched to the limit, and I had given them a talking to at the end of the day. Even Donny had been testing me that day. Quite sharply, I told him to go out to the car and wait for me.

Fifteen minutes later I came out to my 1939 Chevy and saw him sitting there. I felt a little guilty for having spoken so sharply to him. As I started the car Donny turned to me with those innocent blue eyes, and sighing deeply he said in his Danish dialect, "You know, Mr. Petrik, this teaching sure must be the shits!"

Virgil D. Petrik, Vlasak School District #27,
Bon Homme County, SD, 1949-50

IT WAS LATE FALL OF 1955, and I was a 20-year-old, brand new schoolteacher. I had just graduated from Wessington Springs Junior College and had also just recently married. I was teaching in a school seven miles from town and was very excited about my new career.

Just before school one day, I sent two of the boys out to put the flag up. The boys took the folded flag from me and headed out the door. Unbeknown to me, they stopped off first at the outhouse and in a moment accidentally knocked the flag down into the toilet. Needless to say, they felt very sad and were indeed apologetic when they broke the news to me.

I knew that the farmers, the parents of the students for miles around, looked to the school to see that the flag was up—which meant that all was well. Being new on the job, young and inexperienced, I worried throughout the day, and since it was Friday, on into the weekend. I was sure that I could not face the school board president with the details of the missing flag.

By Sunday afternoon my new husband had convinced me that we should drive out to the school board president's home and relate the story. Wanting to get past the episode before another school day, I did just that.

Fortunately, the president was extremely sensitive and kind. After a short discussion, we decided that the money to replace the flag should come from the boys and the Y.C.L. treasury. I left there feeling a great deal better than when I had come.

Dixie Young, Dale Center School,
Jerauld County, SD, 1955-56

OCCASIONALLY, BECAUSE OF ACCUMULATED SOOT IN THE CHIMNEY, the oil stove would "belch," and soot would fly over the schoolroom, covering everything with a black film. One day, a little first grade boy, as blond as blond could be, was standing by my desk getting help when the stove decided to "belch." That poor student was instantly black-headed and covered with grime. The whole school was stunned into silence, but when Jim turned around, we burst into laughter at how comical he looked. Needless to say, school had to be dismissed, and one student and I had the dubious honor of cleaning the whole school from top to bottom!

Sandra A. Dyson, Sperlich School,
Aurora County, 1961-62

All God's Creatures

ONE MORNING, I ARRIVED TO FIND a Shetland pony in my schoolroom. Gail, my sixth grader, had led him up the steps and into the schoolroom! Yes, my pupils all thought I should let him visit until recess, but after I saw him running, jumping and playing with my pupils, I decided recess was too far off.

Florence Lewton Gunn, Maltby School,
Perkins County, SD, 1930-31

IN THE FALL OF 1936, after one year at Notre Dame Junior College in Mitchell, I began teaching a two-family school at Fort Sully. It was in the Missouri River bottom about thirty miles northwest of Pierre. This is now covered by Lake Oahe.

The first morning in my new surroundings, I looked out at a herd of buffalo that had wandered down the river from Sutton's Ranch at Agar. In the winter, airplanes buzzed overhead looking for coyotes. The children knew how to kill a rattlesnake before it could strike.

Magdalena Schmidt Kyte, Fort Sully School,
Sully County, SD, 1936-37

IT ALL HAPPENED DURING OUR LUNCH BREAK while we were seated at our desks. There was an unusually soft, tumbling sound, followed by questioning glances around the room. There on the floor behind the teacher's chair, a bunch of tiny whitish pink baby mice had tumbled out of our bookshelves! Where did that mother mouse have her nest? It was an interruption in lunch, to be sure. There was great excitement, and everyone wanted a baby mouse for a pet!

Ellen Reisdorph Hieb, Heier School,
McPherson County, SD, 1956-1957

I WAS TEACHING IN A ONE-ROOM SCHOOL IN BRULE COUNTY in the fall of 1960. The school was a small wooden structure with a porch. A tall, dark green metal cabinet covered a hole in the porch floor. I had my desk positioned opposite the cabinet and doorway. One day while teaching class, I looked out into the porch, and there sat a groggy gray mouse. It had gotten into the yellow cardboard box of poison that the mothers who cleaned had placed there.

I warned the students there was a mouse in the doorway and told the two older boys to get rid of it. Bedlam took over! The mouse started toward me, and I squatted on the seat of the teacher's chair, and the girls climbed on their desks. All the boys chased the mouse, not just the two who had been asked to! One student found a straw broom on the porch. I remember the scramble, but I don't remember what happened to the poisoned mouse. The outside burning barrel was probably a fitting deathbed.

This was my first encounter with a mouse in a school. For the duration of my two years there, textbooks, True Blue Spellers, construction paper and other art supplies would be chewed by mice who found their way into the supply cabinet.

Patricia Nelson, Bode School,
Brule County, SD, 1960

WE ALL KNEW ABOUT GOPHERS. While some of the more erudite may have called them thirteen-stripe ground squirrels or flickertails, to us they were gophers, pure and simple. These were not the dreaded pocket gophers, whose mounded piles of dirt from their subterranean excavations left a pasture's surface soft enough to collapse over a running horse, breaking legs. Most of us had long since been equipped with .22 caliber rifles, and knew how to shoot them to collect our dad's nickel-a-gopher bounty offer. But you don't bring a rifle to school, and our one-acre schoolground was a haven for gophers. Our problem was to develop a successful method to bring about a reduction in the numbers of gophers on the schoolgrounds.

We found a rusty shovel in the school's basement, a relic from the not-too-distant days before LP-gas furnaces, and we tried digging out the gophers. We took turns on the shovel, each to the limit of his strength, but our only achievement was to ruin part of our kitten-ball diamond. Brownie, the neighbor's dog, hated gophers too, but a mastiff/shepherd/St. Bernard/traveler-cross dog, while suitable for pulling sleds and being an all-around companion, is really not the weapon of choice when it comes to catching gophers.

Then we found a bucket in the road ditch. This bucket had evidently been shot up and smashed by several vehicles, but using our shovel handle, we were able to pry it back to a reasonable shape. At the school pump, we could fill it just to the bullet-holes and then run to the gopher hole. Once the water had been poured into the hole, we crowded 'round, each holding our weapon of choice, ready to bash the gopher the instant his head should appear above the water.

Sometimes it took more than one bucket of water. Sometimes the gopher had an escape hole. But enough times to make it worth our while, a gopher would emerge from the hole and try to scramble through our assembled forces. Then the chase was on.

It was a miracle that none of us hit each other in our eagerness to get the gopher and claim the nickel. Our school was on a gravelled county road. Sometimes the gopher would head across the road with the entire student body in wide-eyed, yelling pursuit. All the teacher's admonitions about watching for traffic were forgotten in our blood lust. By mutual agreement, when the gopher crossed through the fenceline on the far side of the road, it had escaped. Nobody wanted to mess with those cows!

Did we ever kill any gophers? Yes, we did. Not many, but a few. And perhaps we discouraged other gophers from making our playground their residence. We spent many recesses engaged in this loud and energetic endeavor, knowing that every gopher we killed was one less gopher to raid the cornfields.

William A. Justice, Eureka School District 56,
Brookings County, SD, 1946-54

AN EARLY SPRING DAY IN RURAL SOUTH DAKOTA is always wonderful. The smell of new grass, the bleating of the baby lambs and calves, and the increased activity of local wildlife heralds the growing season. One such day, after the children and I had eaten our box lunches and the children were outside playing softball, I decided to pick out the tune to an unfamiliar song the students needed to know for the county music festival. I was not a pianist or organist, but I could, with one hand, pick out the melody on the old pump organ which stood at the entryway of the school.

Then afternoon classes began. The two sixth graders, one fifth, one fourth, one third, and two second grade girls were all busily working in their reading workbooks. The six first graders were up front on the bench for their reading class. Then the unmistakable aroma of skunk filled our peaceful classroom.

All rational thought escaped me. A sixth grade girl and I grabbed a broom and a baseball bat and headed for the basement. A confrontation with a skunk so armed would have been a total disaster, but fortunately, we encountered nothing in the basement. Meanwhile, the other sixth grade girl was busy attempting to calm the younger children. Although we found nothing in the basement, we did find a hole in the landing.

When we re-entered the classroom, we found twelve students standing on their desks with their eyes watering, and a couple of the younger students were in tears. I gently opened the door to the entry where our coats were hung and our lunch boxes were in a row on the floor and where the organ stood. Then the aroma hit me full in the face, and we knew the exact location of our visitor.

The two sixth grade girls, with assistance, crawled out the window. They ran to a home about a quarter mile away to call parents, who arrived shortly. I would have helped the smaller children to escape out the window too, but it was still chilly, and our coats were in the smelly entry. So we waited inside with the windows wide open.

When the parents arrived, school was dismissed for the day. They grabbed coats and lunch boxes and carted us all home, letting the skunk calm down.

Later that evening two or three of the fathers went to the school and dragged the organ out onto the steps and beat on it until the skunk escaped into the night. They then put an odor-absorbing light bulb in the entry and left it on all night. The following day we enjoyed an unexpected vacation.

Mary Valentine Bedsaul, Valley School,
Hyde County, SD, 1953

IT WAS A HOT OCTOBER DAY and I had all the doors and windows open. While we were having a class, a huge rattlesnake came crawling across the floor. The children all screamed and stood on their desks. This scared the snake, and it went into the hallway. I shut the door so it couldn't get out. The snake tried to crawl into the coal bin, but it was too big to get between the slats. One of the boys got me a ball bat, and while the snake was trying to get in the coal bin, I killed it. At this time, the state had a rattlesnake trapper by the name of Dick Jacoby who lived only a few miles from the school. The next day, he came and found a rattlesnake den only a few rods from the schoolhouse.

Later, as a safety measure, the school board got me a rattle-snake kit which included suction cup, sharp knife, tourniquet, disinfectant, and instructions on how to use it. I put this kit on the wall in plain sight. The pupils and I went over the instructions together so we would all know how to use the kit in case of emergency. Fortunately, we never had to use it.

Harold Benson, Greenfield School, 1936-41

ONE FALL MORNING I went to the outdoor toilet before school. The five children were all playing in the schoolyard. After I got seated on the toilet, I heard a rattlesnake rattle. I then noticed a rattlesnake coiled up in a corner of the toilet near the door. Boy! It didn't take me long to get out of there! How the kids did laugh!

Thelma Bucholz Sayler, Cottonwood School,
Mellette County, SD, 1953-54

ONE DAY AT RECESS, one of my third grade girls burst from the outhouse, pulling up her pants and screaming, "Snake!" Upon investigation, I determined that a rattlesnake was under the floor of the toilet. I found a post for a lever and raised a corner of the structure. Sure enough, there was the rattler. I couldn't extract the snake and run the lever, so I asked the seventh grade boy to help.

He was not strong enough to run the pry pole, so I ran the pole and gave him the shovel to remove the snake with. The outhouse was near maximum capacity. In the struggle, the boy got the snake into the pit. After several attempts at removing the snake from the pit, he was finally successful. I then grabbed the shovel and killed the snake.

That was one mad rattlesnake!

Leo Giacometto, Hay Creek School,
Carter, MT, 1976-77

Eyeing the Storm

IT HAD RAINED VERY LITTLE, and the winds had dried out the soil, causing frequent dust storms, as they came to be called. I remember one dust storm in particular on a Friday afternoon. That day had dawned calm and bright, but soon dark clouds began to form. It was hard to see if they were rain clouds or dust clouds. Then the wind began blowing and it grew so dark and dusty that concerned parents came for their children. The dust was so thick it was hard to breathe. As I remember, it continued to blow all night, and dust sifted in wherever there was a crack.

When I got back to the school building on Monday morning and opened the door, dust crunched under my shoes. Everything had to be cleaned and dusted and the floor had to be swept before we could begin classes. The smell of dust was everywhere.

Gladys Brewick, Sanborn County, SD, 1930s

THE WORST YEAR I TAUGHT WAS THE 1933-34 TERM at the Miles School. It was a dry summer and fall, no rain, and the dirt began to blow. Each day the wind seemed to blow harder; everywhere there was dirt, inside and out. No longer could you sweep the floor after school for the next morning; before you could have school that day, everything had to be cleaned. Many days the dirt blew so hard and thick that you could not see the blackboards nor one another across the room. Soon after dinner, the parents would come for their children. It was necessary to drive with lights on and hope you could drive through the drifts of dirt on the roads; and you would hope not to meet another car. Of course, the children liked these short days of school just as children today like to be dismissed because of a snowstorm. The next morning, complete cleaning would have to be done again, only to realize that the next day would be the same.

No rain, no feed, no crops—but one crop was grasshoppers; they were everywhere. They hit you as you walked or rode, spitting their tobacco on your clothes. They were on buildings, roads, fields, railroad tracks, everywhere. They ate everything and cleaned all vegetation clean, except for the Russian Thistles. Your cars would slip on the roads where they were thick. The Milwaukee & St. Louis Railroad track went from Conde into the hills to Watertown. Sometimes the train had difficulty getting up the hills for slipping on the grasshoppers on the tracks.

But the rugged and determined South Dakota people always looked for a better tomorrow and a brighter new year. With the help of the government W.P.A. projects and sharing and working together, the people survived the dirty thirties and the Depression.

Helen Borwell Rossow Miles School,
Spink County, SD, 1933-34

THE WINTER OF 1936 we had a very severe snowstorm. It was six weeks before a car could get through. What a thrill to see the first horse and hayrack that Sunday morning! I set my clock by the sun and managed some semblance of time. When the year began, there were two families with children in school. Soon the children of only one family remained.

Magdalena Schmidt Kyte, Fort Sully School,
Sully County, SD, 1936-37

THE SCHOOL NEVER HAD A PHONE, so our parents never knew if we got to school or not. When there was a snowstorm, I walked down to the neighbors, and their father hooked up a horse and wagon, and we crawled down in the hay to stay warm and put towels over our faces to keep from freezing. He would take us to school, and then come back and get us.

Faye Bertram, Turtle Butte School,
Tripp County, SD, 1945

IN THE EARLY 1930s I lived at what was then known as the Brown County Poor Farm, where my mother was the matron. My father went to his job in town. As a result, I attended Plainview Demonstration School. It was a one-room schoolhouse about five miles east of Aberdeen.

Northern Normal's professors of education used this school to try out their new methods of teaching. Plainview was aptly named, for it was a white frame building alone in the middle of the prairie, without a tree or shrub in sight.

One winter was especially severe, with roads closed by snow drifts so high and frozen so hard that even the largest snow-plows could not break them up. Miss Keller, our teacher, could not get to school the usual way, nor could I. However, we could each get to a certain farm where the owner had a big sled and a team of Belgian horses. The teacher didn't want to close school, and my parents didn't want me to miss classes, so it was decided that it was possible for us to stay at the school a week at a time. So on Sunday afternoons we were carried in the big sled over the snow-covered fields to the school, where we would remain until the next Friday afternoon.

We were fortunate that this school had a small stage with big doors that could be closed off from the main classroom. It was there that we set up our cots. We also had the unheard of luxury of a telephone, a furnace, indoor chemical toilets and a cooking range in the basement. However, there we were for a week at a time as the wind and snow swirled around the school, and each night the groans of the wood frame structure were a terror to me—a nine-year-old girl who had never been away from her parents until then. The farmer and his beautiful team each Friday were such a welcome sight, as I looked forward to the tomato and mayonnaise sandwich that my mother always promised me. That doesn't seem like much of a treat, but in the 1930s on the prairie, it was true luxury. Miss Keller was a dedicated teacher to isolate herself for a week at a time to keep her school open and put up with a nine-year-old.

Jeanne Biegler Roers, Plainview Demonstration School, Brown County, SD, 1931

THE WHOLE SCHOOL where I taught would go outside for recess, including me. One day it began to snow, and by noon we had a blizzard. No one could go home. What a long day! We had to pump a bucket of water. We all held hands to go to the well. Some big boys carried in wood. I was worried about a fire, as the wind blew so hard that chimney was red hot. We finally had dinner, as the school board had put in a few groceries, just in case. I read a book for awhile to the students. At bedtime, we shoved seats together, and they slept on them with no pillows or blankets. Going to the bathroom was a problem. I'd take the girls into the hall, and we used a little bucket. The boys did the same. We had an outhouse out back, but we couldn't get to it. By morning we were glad to see the parents.

Blanche Keller, Dalton School,
Pennington County, SD, 1932

WHEN I WAS IN THE EIGHTH GRADE, we had a very bad blizzard. Dad always took us to school with sled and horses. By afternoon the weather had become threatening, so we had to stay at the school overnight. At first we thought it was fun, but when it became dark and the wind was howling fiercely and we were getting hungry, then it got scary. But we made it through the night with the help of our good teacher, and by morning the storm had subsided and Dad had come with breakfast and lunch for the day. We were very happy to see him and thankful that he was all right, as we had worried that he was caught in the storm.

LaVera Rall, Harrison #1 School,
McPherson County, SD, 1935-36

ONE TIME IN MY SEVENTH GRADE, we had a terrible snowstorm, and it was still blowing pretty hard in the morning. I was the oldest of the girls, and my dad tied a rope around my middle, with the other two girls tied onto it. Dad made us walk along the fence line, holding on to the wire for dear life. But this route was a mile, and so it took longer to get to school, plus every so often we had to thaw out our gloves to keep them from sticking to the wire. We were pretty well tired out by the time we finally got to school. To our horror, the teacher did not show up, and we couldn't get a fire started in the stove, so after about an hour we decided to head on home. It was only by the grace of God that we made it. Dad met us about halfway. By this time, we were completely disoriented.

Clara M. Hoffer, McPherson County, SD, 1940-41

ON JANUARY 2 the weather looked pretty threatening, so my brother Dick and I, who were the youngest, got to stay home. The others rode on to school, but according to our brothers, John and Lyle, they hadn't been there long before it started getting unusually dark out, and a few snowflakes started falling. So the teacher decided to send everyone home early. By the time they were all dressed to go, the weather was much worse.

They should have stayed in the school that night, but they decided instead to go to the nearest farm, which was only a quarter mile west and then south up a long driveway. The smaller children were put on horses, and the teacher and the older boys walked.

They were headed west right into the storm, which was getting worse by the minute. It wasn't long before they couldn't see the ground or even the horses they were hanging on to. John was supposed to be leading the horses, but by then he was just hanging on to the reins. Everyone who could was to watch for the gatepost to the farmer's driveway, which had a yellow sign nailed to it. But finally it seemed that they had been on the road too long and must have gone past the driveway.

By then everyone was scared, and some were crying, including the teacher. If they had gone past the driveway, they had better try to turn the horses around. But what if they hadn't gone far enough? This might just confuse the horses. John was certain they had gone too far, so when the horses finally started to turn south, he thought it must be the section-line road.

About that time Lyle thought he saw a glimpse of the yellow sign, and if that was true, they were headed up the farmer's driveway. Sure enough, a little while later the horses came to a stop right in front of the gate to the house. Everyone had made it, with only a little frostbite here and there, and they were a lot wiser. Luckily, the horses had been up and down that road many times hauling drinking water for the school, and so they knew just where they were going, even if they couldn't see.

Alden Gillings, McKay School District 2,
Charles Mix County, SD, 1937

THE WINTER OF 1936-37 WAS VERY SEVERE. I was teaching at the McFarland School in Yankton County. This school had a basement with a coal-burning furnace. One day a terrific blizzard hit the area. Dismissal time approached and I realized that the storm was life-threatening. Some parents, fearing that a bad storm was eminent, had come earlier in the day to get their children, but I spent the night at school with thirteen pupils. There were no telephones, and parents had to trust in my judgment to keep the children at school. A kind farmer who lived near the school followed the fence line, bringing us some food and blankets. The children slept on the floor with their coats on, while I kept vigil over the furnace. It was a long night, but at daybreak, the wind diminished, and fathers braved the huge snowdrifts and sub-zero weather to rescue us with horse-drawn wagons and sleighs.

Pauline Kjergaard, McFarland School,
Yankton County, SD, 1936-37

MY BROTHER BUD AND I ALWAYS WALKED TO SCHOOL across the fields. In the winter you would get awful cold with the wind and snow blowing in your face, so lots of times we walked backward to the wind. It wasn't long before I came up with a bright idea for keeping my head warm. I used a cardboard box bigger than my head and cut a hole in it at eye level. Then I put isinglass in the hole so I'd be able to see out. One of the other school kids, Elmer, saw me coming to school with the box on my head, and he wondered what that Rawden kid had come up with now. I'm sure it probably looked kinda strange, but it worked to keep my face from freezing. Some fifty years later, Elmer still remembered this incident and wondered if I remembered when I came to school with a box over my head!

Delbert Rawden, Chambers School,
Faulk County, SD, 1925-30

The Social Calendar

WHEN I THINK ABOUT ATTENDING OUR ONE-ROOM SCHOOL in the '50s, I always think of the holidays. The first major one was Halloween. During the week before the party, the sixth through eighth graders sealed off the basement from the view of the other students. They assembled a maze of sorts using the Christmas stage curtains. Then, the afternoon of the party, grapes were peeled for "eyeballs," an assortment of noodles was cooked and cooled for "innards," and garlic water squirt guns were prepared for the "bats' breath." As the party began, the younger kids were individually blindfolded and escorted through the "House of Horrors," feeling the surprises and hearing all sorts of ghoulish sounds.

We also always had the traditional costume party. One year we were all stumped, when during the afternoon the front door opened, and in filed silent, adult, costumed people. They circled the room, and our teacher, acting as if she did not know what was going on, asked our help in identifying the intruders. Most of us were embarrassed and amazed that we hadn't even recognized our own mothers!

Before Halloween, any neighbor who wanted trick-or-treaters would call the school. That night we would meet at the school, along with parents and our younger siblings, to form a caravan to the prearranged homes. We were always welcomed into the houses, where we unmasked and introduced ourselves. The treats we were given were usually homemade, and very generous amounts. I remember that if it was a real cold evening and we had to wear our winter coats under our costumes, we got uncomfortably hot while in the houses and couldn't wait until we were able to run outside, always shouting one last "thank you!"

Right after Thanksgiving, preparations for the Christmas season began. The teacher would hand out pieces to learn; we would practice holiday songs, and rehearse our parts for plays. The room was always decorated from top to bottom, using red and green construction paper chains and brightly-colored, seasonal figures. Blackboard murals were done in colored chalk.

A couple of days before our program, the desks were pushed to the edges of the room, and it was cleaned and cleared of anything small enough for us to take to the basement. The fathers would deliver the wood planks and concrete blocks borrowed from the local lumberyard and assemble them into our stage and audience seating. We had black sheets for our backdrop and heavy brocaded curtains for the front of the stage, with siderooms for changing and staying out of sight when not on stage.

We had a dress rehearsal the afternoon of the program, but it never compared to the performance we gave that night. Arriving in our new Christmas outfits, so scrubbed and groomed, we almost didn't recognize one another. We nervously awaited curtain time. The school would be filled to standing room only with our families, friends and neighbors. We started with the welcome, often done by the youngest student and many times never recited, because of a case of stage fright brought on by the opening of the curtain to reveal the "huge" crowd.

Individual pieces were said, every song was sung, and the main play was performed for the appreciative and biased audience. We always sold raffle tickets prior to the program. A drawing was done, and lunch was served in the basement following our performance.

Leona Anderson McInerney, Peterson Country
School District 73, Union County, SD, 1950s

WEEKS PRIOR TO THE BIG DAY, art projects were begun; and the red and green Santas, bells, reindeer and angels were cut and glued. Plenty of glitter was applied to both the paper and the children. Special gifts were made for all the parents. Some of the skits we presented were humorous. Some would probably not be considered "politically correct" today, as they carried definite religious themes.

One year we presented Charles Dickens' Christmas Carol. Not only could we recite our own parts from memory, but each knew the other parts as well. Everyone from first through eighth grade participated in the play. The teacher, who seemed to be able to rise to any occasion, provided us with a box containing the most wonderful costumes, wigs and other props.

A few days before the program was to be held, the school board members would come to the school to set up the stage, which was crudely built with sawhorses and planks. The two days before the program were devoted to dress rehearsals. We dutifully played our rhythm band instruments and sang along with the teacher as she played on the large upright piano in the back of the room. The piano was always out of tune. As we had no plumbing in the building, it was not kept heated during weekends and vacations.

When the big day finally arrived, the teacher sprinkled red sweeping compound all over the floor, and then gave us permission to slide across it in our shoes. The supposed purpose of the sliding was to work the oily compound into the wood; but I now suspect that it was a diversion to work off her students' energy. After the compound was swept up, the folding chairs were arranged in rows facing the stage.

Melanie L. Parsons, Pleasant Grove School District 58,
Turner County, SD, 1961-69

WHEN IT WAS MY TURN TO SPEAK, I choked for breath, panicked, and ran out of the schoolhouse. I hid in the rear seat area of the family's 1923 automobile. When it was time for popcorn balls, my father, who had watched where I had gone, came out and talked me into coming into the schoolhouse again. The Santa Claus had a paper mache face, which made me wonder why anyone would want to live where it was so cold that his face froze stiff.

Tom Shonley, Long School, Aurora County, SD, 1930-35

EACH CHRISTMAS THE SCHOOL DID A SHOW for the parents and neighbors. There was very little talent in Eddy School. One year Vernon and I did a blackface act. The next year we repeated it in town, but we swapped roles. I don't think a blackface act would be done now.

Gerald Matson, Eddy School,
Jerauld County, SD, 1946-51

IN THE PLAY WAS A FAIRY GODMOTHER, dressed in the beautiful blue dress I wore to my cousin Evelyn's wedding. Other students portrayed humble shepherds and aristocratic wise men, while nervously pulling their belts tighter and rolling up the sleeves one more notch on their fathers' bathrobes. The play was about neighbors and friends, angels and shepherds, Jesus and Santa Claus.

Karen Petersen White, Skyberg School,
Kingsbury County, SD, 1947

WE HAD A FAMILY WHO SUPPORTED THE SCHOOL, but they didn't approve of Christmas. Their children, who wanted to be in the program, were given the job of drawing and closing the curtains and helping with stage props.

One Christmas, my best friend and I decided to sing, acappela, "Silent Night" in English and then in Spanish. Being eleven, we thought that would be terrific, even though we had no Spanish students. The facts that neither of us could sing very well and our Spanish was murdered didn't stop us.

The night of our "fancy" entertainment, as we were struggling through the Spanish, and the audience was politely quiet, I saw my father in the back of the room trying to hang a red paper Christmas bell, with the program inside it, on the ear of a friend sitting in front of him. The string on the bell wasn't very long, and it was hard to get it on the man's big ear.

I tried hard to stop a rising giggle; my friend punched me in my ribs, and how we ever got through "Silent Night" is beyond me!

We always had a visit from Santa Claus. After the program, there was a lunch of sandwiches, cakes, cookies and beverages, and the gift exchange.

There was a bachelor who lived three miles from the schoolhouse. He was small and wiry, and he had black hair and a "cookie duster" mustache. He always rode a big white horse and was usually dressed in his World War I army uniform, with a long sword hanging from his belt.

He tried to hit on every young, pretty teacher we had, but they weren't awed by him.

However, he made a kindly, efficient, but skinny Santa Claus, dressed in a Santa Claus suit. He always brought along a big box of Red Delicious Apples or oranges. Since fruit wasn't very often part of our diets, we were joyous.

There was no electricity, so kerosene lamps and lanterns provided lighting for these evening events.

Rozella Bracewell, Riggs School,
Meade County, SD, 1927-34

I REMEMBER THAT ONE YEAR we were told that Santa was supposed to be coming in a helicopter. It was all pretty real to me as I heard the roar of the helicopter outside. But I found out later that it was just the teacher's boyfriend racing the motor of his car!

Evelyn Myers Sharping, Swanson School,
Brule County, SD, 1930s

WHEN I TAUGHT IN A RURAL SCHOOL before my marriage, I asked Otho, one of the older boys, to dress up as Santa and distribute the presents and candy after the Christmas program. His little sister was in the first grade that year, and while Santa was giving out the presents, she came up to me and said, "Miss Simonson, Santa has a ring just like Otho's!" I don't believe she ever realized that Santa really WAS Otho!

Mary Simonson Thompson, Hanson School District 25,
Brown County, 1941

HOW THRILLING THE CHRISTMAS TREE WAS—towering far above our heads! It was so much larger than anyone had at home, its branches covered with REAL candles. (Our home Christmas tree was a huge tumbleweed which Mother covered with sparkling starch.) We drew names for presents, but we exchanged names again and again to get the name we really wanted. Gradually, packages were sneaked under the pine branches, and candles were checked and double-checked for safety.

The pot-bellied stove cast a warm glow on the proud parents and the restless little brothers and sisters, while the elated students nervously waited behind the curtain. A welcome, poems, songs, and a play were the program. Finally, the big moment came when the teacher and a father lit the little white candles. There was no electricity in the building. Almost by magic, we would hear sleigh bells outside. In Santa would bound, merrily shouting, "Ho! Ho! Ho! Merry Christmas, everyone!" Then he would ask for helpers to distribute the gifts. To each of us he would put the question, "Have you been good this year?"

Before Santa left, he would ceremoniously pull bags of candy from his big brown bag, and then he would bound from the room shouting, "Merry Christmas to all!" We would hear the sound of the sleigh bells growing fainter and fainter as Santa drove his reindeer on the hard-crusted snow. By this time, the candles had to be extinguished. The only glow from the pot-bellied stove would be from the red clinkers. The long-awaited party was over for another year.

Eleanore Rowan Moe, Rowan School,
Sanborn County, SD, 1926-33

WE WERE PRIVILEGED to have a real, roll-up stage curtain with elaborate advertising on it from local merchants. The backdrop was sheets from home, with the dingy ones hung in the back. Everyone brought food and refreshments to share after the production. It was a feast with homemade pies, cakes and sandwiches.

I can still remember the flush of excitement in reciting my monologue, seeing my father's eyes twinkle in the audience, the pride of not having to be prompted, and the sleepy but happy ride home at midnight.

Marilyn Owen, Sunflower School District 112,
Saline County, NE, 1934-39

EACH LADY WOULD DECORATE A BOX, usually a shoe box, and fill it with all sorts of goodies to eat. The identity of the box-maker was kept a secret! These boxes were auctioned off by some man from the neighborhood, and the money taken in would be used by the school for supplies, such as books, maps, globes, and other things. That always was a fun time. I must say, too, that every man who bought a box ate the lunch from that box with the girl or lady who brought it. The teacher's box usually sold for a good price!

Gladys Brewick, Sanborn County, SD, 1930s

I WATCHED MY SISTER wrapping the box with great interest. I was making a mental note of the color of paper and ribbon, because tomorrow at school I knew he would ask me to describe it to him. I was being careful not to look too interested, though. I didn't want her getting suspicious and changing it at the last minute.

I had three older sisters and I suppose they were all getting boxes ready. Our one-room schoolhouse was not only used for school, but for the few social events our parents took time away from the ranch work to attend. For the box social, all women, single or married, made a picnic lunch for two and packed it in a box. Each gal decorated her box as she wished, and when everyone had assembled at the schoolhouse, the men began bidding. After a successful bid was reached on a box, whoever had made that bid stepped forward, and the two of them would go over to the desks and chairs to have their picnic lunch together. It was a fun evening of visiting for everyone. There were always a few unmarried ones of marrying age in the community, so this made the event particularly interesting.

My teacher happened to be a single, good-looking guy, who was very interested in getting acquainted with my older, twenty-something sister. I was being asked to play Cupid and help arrange it so my teacher could end up with my sister's lunch box. I don't remember whether he got the bid and had lunch with my sister or not, but it sure made looking forward to that event exciting.

Mary Giesler, Tip Top School, Corson County, SD, 1964

ONE OF MY MOST UNFORGETTABLE CHRISTMAS CELEBRATIONS was in 1949. I was 18 years old, two years out of high school, and teaching school in a little one-room country school. I had nine pupils scattered from the first grade to the eighth grade.

The stage was set, and the families of the students were packed into the rest of the small room. Everything was ready, but we couldn't start quite yet. You see, my girlfriend was there too, and my boyfriend and her boyfriend had promised they would come to the program, but they hadn't arrived. Everyone was getting restless. Then there came the sound of a car and the door opened and the two guys came in. There was a murmur, for everyone knew the reason for the delay.

Finally the show could go on! My fourth grader Jerry was going to welcome the audience. Two girls were poised to open the curtains. Suddenly into the hushed silence of the room came an anguished stage whisper: "Miss Brown! Miss Brown! My pants are falling down!" The room filled with laughter as I hurried behind the curtains to see Jerry desperately trying to keep up a new pair of pants which were too big for him.

After a quick search for a safety pin, we got the falling trousers anchored safely, and this time the show actually did go on. The pupils did a good job with their songs, plays, etc., and were given a good hand of applause.

Then it was time for lunch. We had planned a basket social to raise some money to buy a phonograph and some records for the school. The two boyfriends had been previously informed of the appearance of our baskets so they would be sure to buy the right ones. With one of the neighbor men acting as auctioneer, the sale began.

He held up the first ribboned basket and asked for a bid. Somebody bid a dollar, somebody else bid $2, $3, $4; and just as the auctioneer was about to say "sold," my boyfriend raised the bid. The other bidder, somewhat surprised, raised the bid again. So did my boyfriend. I watched in shocked surprise as the basket was handed to him. It wasn't mine! He looked at me and grinned and winked. I smiled back, still wondering what was going on.

The auctioneer held up the second basket and asked for bids. Just as he was about to say "sold!" my girlfriend's boyfriend started to bid and raised it until he too had a basket.

The third basket was held up, and the bidding started. After a few bids, my boyfriend started bidding again and in no time he had two baskets.

The fourth basket was held up, and the husband of the basket's owner started the bidding. A couple of other tentative bids were heard, and then my girlfriend's boyfriend began to bid, and then he had two baskets. So far, nobody else had any.

Whispers ran around the room, what were those guys trying to do, anyway? Did they intend to buy all the baskets? And if so, why?

Another whisper ran around the room. Ok, if they wanted all the baskets, they'd have to pay for them.

When the rest of the baskets were sold, it was the other men raising the bids, but in the end, most of the baskets were stacked in front of our guys, and they had to pay a substantial price for all of them.

Then with everyone still wondering what was going on and if they should be mad or what, my boyfriend explained that they had just bought the baskets to be sure we made enough money for the school, and then they each picked out our baskets and said to the people, "There they are! Help yourselves."

Well, in no time, everyone was eating and talking and laughing, and the evening was a big success.

That boyfriend has been my husband for forty some years now.

Lavonne L. Crook, Heer School,
Spink County, SD, 1949-50

WHEN I GOT TO THE LONE TREE LAKE SCHOOL, I learned about the basket social at Christmas time. I learned about that about the same time that I noticed girls. Unfortunately, I didn't make out too good the first couple of years. Then I attended a Christmas program with a basket social at one of the other schools in the area.

There I met my dream girl. But I struck out again, due to insufficient funds. So on the 26th of December, I began planning for the next year. The next time, I was the top bidder, although it cost me the equivalent of what a lobster dinner for two costs today. But it was a barrel of fun. The money went for a good cause. Those Christmas programs and basket socials were very good get-togethers. The students learned to work and play together. These events also got the parents together, which made it more like one, big, happy family than just a neighborhood.

Dick Deboer, Lone Tree Lake School, SD, 1940-42

FEBRUARY BROUGHT A SHOWER OF RED HEARTS! The children made many Valentines for the teacher, parents and fellow pupils. A large box was decorated, and as the valentines were made, they were dropped into the box to await Valentine's Day. On February 14th, the mothers would come to school, bringing lunch and treats for all. They would watch with glee as their children received the pretty hearts.

Violet Paschke Scherer, Clear Lake School District 67,
Minnehaha County, SD, 1943-44

ONCE OUR DISTRICT HEADS decided to join with the district to the north for an end-of-the-year picnic at their schoolyard. Everyone brought yummy eats at noon that day, probably a Sunday. For entertainment we had pieces to say, and I, being quite good at drawing, was to draw a picture on the blackboard. So I did, a picture of a pretty Colonial lady. I was applauded.

After dinner, a baseball game was played. Bigger boys and young men were pitted against the fellows from the other district. The game was going well when a ball was socked for a homer. A young man on second base made a dash for third and home, when we all heard a sharp CRACK like a rifle shot—the young man had stepped into a gopher hole and broken his leg!

Somebody started up their car and took the poor guy to Sioux Falls to a doctor or maybe to a hospital. We had no more such neighborhood picnics.

Myra Kalb, District 71 School,
Minnehaha County, SD, 1926

THE FINAL EVENT OF THE YEAR was the picnic the last day of school. As the final cleaning of the school was accomplished and we labored through final tests, our thoughts were drawn to the outdoors. Windows were open and flies buzzed against the windowpanes. Someone usually got stung by a wasp or a bee to create a small emergency. There were tall cottonwood trees across the road from our school, and the bluejays called to each other all day. Now when I hear their distinctive squawk, the feeling of school days comes back to me. If there was no wind, the building heated up until our arms stuck to our papers and we longed for a shady yard. Some days we got so drowsy we'd almost fall asleep.

But at last the big day arrived. Everyone brought piles of food, and the whole family came. Dad was always reluctant to give up farming time in the field, but this was an important day and he usually came. All the men would play ball with the boys. Sometimes the girls played too, and it was such fun. We loved seeing our dads running those bases. Some kids were surprised that their dads were so athletic. A few dads went home with very sore muscles from such unaccustomed activities! The food was the best. We ate and played until it was chore time, and everyone went home. I'm sure the teacher heaved a great sigh of relief when the last carload of families left. Mothers, little kids and most girls sat on the sidelines and gossiped and cheered the boys on. I never knew whether I wanted to play or sit and listen to the older ladies talk. It was all so informative!

Phylis Brunken, Law School,
Douglas County, SD, 1934-42

Testimonials

THE COUNTRY SCHOOLS gave us a good education and they were the foundation of the community.

Ida DeNeui Poppenga, Ashlawn District 89,
Turner County, SD, 1925-33

MY METHODS TEACHER AT AUGUSTANA COLLEGE often reminded us that when we closed that schoolroom door, we should remember that we were responsible not only for the minds of the children, but for the physical well-being and the spirit of each child. Shaking her finger at us, she said emphatically, "Don't quench the spirit!"

This counsel proved to be a great gift to my teaching.

The longer I taught, the more I disliked driving and the temperamental South Dakota weather, but I enjoyed teaching to the very end.

Astrid Raad, Augustana College,
Sioux Falls, SD, 1939-40

I'LL ALWAYS BLESS MY 6TH, 7TH AND 8TH GRADE TEACHER, Grace Buell, of Sioux Falls. She urged us to always do our best. She saw what our talents were and encouraged us to develop them.

Myra Dubbe Kalb, District 71 School,
Minnehaha County, SD, 1925-28

IN THE THIRTIES, the younger children finished their work a week earlier than the seventh and eighth graders, who were to use that last week for review for their final exams. That last week of one school year, there were only eight of us in the school, four eighth graders, three seventh graders and me. At recess and at noon they wanted to play ball, as usual. They had a conference among themselves and then came to ask me if I would play ball with them. I said, "Yes, that would be fun." So we were off to the ball diamond. The spokesman for the group told me to stand on first base, and if the batter hit a ball near first, I was supposed to catch it and put the player out. He gave me a glove and showed me how to use it. So I put it on as he said, and stood on first base. The first batter up hit the ball right in my direction. I reached up my hand—the one without the glove—and caught it! It stunned all of them. Then all seven of them came running to me saying, "Miss Brewick, why haven't you been playing with us all year!" Our review week was good, and our ball games were better and better everyday. Why hadn't I played ball with them all during the season? We had fun, and I learned to know them better than I had all year! A teacher and her pupils can be good friends, and we were.

Gladys Brewick, Sanborn County, SD, 1930s

I DON'T REGRET ANY OF THE EXPERIENCES I had as a one-room school teacher because I can't help but feel it made me more ready to be a wife and mother when I got married. None of us then thought too much about the hardships and sacrifices we made, but tried to do our very best to provide an education for the children we had the privilege to have under our care. Looking back, my only hope is that all of those I had under my care have good memories, because even though sometimes it was difficult, it was a good experience.

Ruth I. Foster, Thorpe School,
Perkins County, SD, 1938-39

JUST THINK OF ALL THE FUN we had and I even got paid for it. The whole sum of $50 a month. And the county superintendent thought I had the hardest school in the county. It was there that I met my husband-to-be, Fred Nelson.

Emma Sittner Nelson, Chance School,
Perkins County, SD, 1939

ONCE A YEAR there was a Teacher's Institute at the county seat. On this day, usually a Saturday, there were lectures, demonstrations and displays of teaching materials. I believe that during my first year, the county superintendent recognized how disheartening our low salaries were, for we had a speaker who challenged us to learn a few beautiful lines of verse each day and to keep our eyes searching for something lovely, until we could say to ourselves, "Isn't that beautiful!" We were given small notebooks in which to copy the poems she taught us. The first was this poem by Sara Teasdale:

> Into my heart's treasury
> I slipped a coin
> That time cannot take
> Nor a thief purloin—
> Oh, better than the minting
> Of a gold-crowned king
> Is the safe-kept memory
> Of a lovely thing.

Myrtle Hundstad Mortimer,
Edmunds County, SD, 1932-33

THE TEACHERS OF THOSE ONE-ROOM COUNTRY SCHOOLS have never received the praise most of them deserved. It was not easy teaching eight grades with students of assorted abilities while covering all the subjects now taught by several different teachers—not only reading, writing, arithmetic, geography, history, spelling, etc., but also music and art. Most of the students that I went to country school with were very able to compete with students who graduated from urban schools, which I think speaks well for our teachers.

I have never regretted that my first experience with school was in the one-room country schoolhouse, though at the time, I probably thought I was deprived.

Ardelle A. Lundeen, Alban School District 2, 1935-41

WHAT NOW SEEMS MOST IMPORTANT about the old-time school is that it gave even the beginner a sense of purpose. Next year he would be in that class that was doing things he couldn't do at present. I don't remember any complaints about school then or students hating to go to school.

Mary Magirl Dougherty, Clearview School,
Tripp County, SD, 1944-50

MY SON AND DAUGHTER WERE BOTH IN SCHOOL when an opportunity arose for me to be county superintendent, so I agreed to supervise the rural schools. The job was fun, and having to visit all the schools at least twice a year gave me a good insight into how wonderfully the one-room school could shape the students. I am convinced that with the right teacher, there is no better atmosphere for a good foundation in learning and no better opportunity for helping younger students who need a little guidance. Sitting in the classroom and hearing the other students have class recitation reinforces what you have learned, or gives you an insight into new information. By the time you finish 8th grade, you are well-grounded in the basics and ready to head for high school.

Betty Larrington, Potter County, SD, 1956-70

WE DIDN'T HAVE ELECTRICITY, no radios, no TVs, poor roads, not many telephones—but we had our schools.

Eva Madden, Beadle County Superintendent, late 1920s-30s

WE DID LEARN OUR ABCS, we did learn our multiplication tables, and we did learn at Eddy School without special classes or computers. We mainly learned because of our teachers and the fact that we were expected to learn by our parents and our community.

Gerald Matson, Eddy School,
Jerauld County, SD, 1946-51

SIMPLE TIMES, SIMPLE PLEASURES. They wouldn't thrill today's children. But they were our lives and we enjoyed them.

Gertrude Johnson, Howard School District 140,
Minnehaha County, SD, 1936-40

EVERYONE FROM OUR SCHOOL BECAME SUCCESSFUL. Probably not geniuses on Wall Street, but we all had realistic goals and achieved them. We supported ourselves and raised great families. We always have wonderful funny nostalgic stories to visit about when we see each other, and of course they grow into taller tales with age.

Pat Speelman, Wayne School District 3,
Hanson County, SD, 1940s

THE ONE-ROOM SCHOOL TAUGHT LOYALTY to our country in the raising of the flag each day. It taught responsibility in taking care of assigned duties. It taught compassion and caring in the helping of younger students. It also taught respect for the teacher and each other and for each others' belongings.

Ideals were developed and carried on into adult lives. The moral and ethical ideals of many of our country's leaders were developed in little rural schools.

Louise Ranek, McCrea School,
Bon Homme County, SD, 1930-32

HAVE WE LOST, through the clutter and chaos of "state of the art" learning tools, the orderliness, innovation and inventiveness that frugality and austerity foster?

As we hasten to fill the tiny heads of today's children with all the world's great knowledge, might we also teach them the wisdom of the innocence of yesterday's children?

Knowledge and wisdom are not the same!

Mary Ann Rager, Howard and Hillview-Sleepy Hollow
Schools, Yankton County, SD, 1946-50

ONE ROOM SCHOOLHOUSE

IN RETROSPECT, the beneficial features of the one-room school were the personal attention from the teacher, plus being able to listen in on the other grades' instructions. It allowed one to learn from the higher grades early on, and then later on to review from the lower grades. It made learning much more interesting. There was essentially nothing wrong with one-room schools. There was a lot right about them. They provided a fine education in tolerance and respect for your peers and the teacher's personal attention for book learning. Students really cared for, and about each other, and the teacher was respected and loved.

Donald E. Buss, Fiddle Creek School,
Fall River County, SD, 1920-21

THE ONE THING I REALLY WOULD LIKE PEOPLE TO KNOW about country schools is they are a wonderful learning environment. This goes for the students, teachers and parents. There is a closeness that can never be severed between students and families because of this experience. I only hope that I have touched the students' lives as much as they have touched mine.

Sandy Sivertsen, Como School,
Hand County, SD, 1996-98

E p i l o g u e

HOSKINS SCHOOL was located in Theresa Township, Beadle County, about two miles west and one mile north of Huron, South Dakota. Our sons, Wayne and Vern Lindblad, attended this school just a few years before it closed.

When it closed in the early seventies, it was used for a township hall and a meeting place for elections. But through the years, vandals almost destroyed it. They broke windows out and tore down light fixtures and anything they could get ahold of. Our sons were upset that their little country school was being vandalized and wondered if the building could be purchased and restored.

We thought it was a great idea, so when the local township decided to sell the school and opened bids, we knew exactly what we wanted to do. In 1975, we contacted the South Dakota Fair Board and asked them if they would like to have a one-room school to be placed on the fairgrounds. They were very pleased and agreed to pay for the moving.

Our two sons, in order to come up with the money to purchase the school, decided to sell their 4-H calves, and when the school went up for bids, the boys put in their bid. Theirs was the only bid received, so the school was theirs. They asked their Uncle Frank Bootz, who was a house mover, to move it for them. It was moved and set down about a block west of the Fair office on Third Street in Huron, right next to the Dakotaland Museum.

Local people in Huron were very willing to supply all the materials to help restore the school to its original condition. Green Thumbers painted the school and restored all the windows, doors, etc. Other people donated furniture, books, desks, etc., to help restore the interior.

The school is now on display during the fair. Fairgoers can enter and see what a schoolhouse looked like when one teacher taught all eight grades.

Carl and Verla Lindblad, Hoskins School,
Beadle County, SD, 1975

I HAD GONE TO A SCHOOL where two grades were held in each classroom, and I had read the *Little House on the Prairie* books like every good elementary school student does, but country school was something foreign to me when I started teaching six years ago. On an early September day in 1992, I walked up the freshly scrubbed entry stairs to the 18' x 28' classroom, and into the lives of thirteen students, grades 5 through 8.

Though I had spent months preparing for this day, I was more than a little frightened, and I had no idea what the next 180 school days would hold. My students smiled at me, and I began the task of telling a little about myself, explaining the day's schedule, and finding out something about each of the kids before me. They ranged in age from 12 to 16 years (two of the boys had been held back), and all but two of the six boys were as tall as me or taller. A couple of the girls were too, and they were all a bit shy about having a "man" teacher, just as I was shy about being one.

That first day flew by and the daily challenge of beating the clock began. A few days into the schedule, I discovered that I had assigned most of the classes to the wrong books, or to work they had done several times with their former teacher. I was always out of time; my explanations made no sense; my examples didn't turn out right; and at the end of the day, my brain felt like it had been thrown in a blender from answering so many questions about so many different things. Throughout all the days of mistakes, my students sat patiently by, helping me when I asked for help, and gently teaching me how things had been done before. To my surprise, they never complained and they seemed to know that I was trying my best to figure things out.

I didn't even see the end of the school year coming because everything was so new and so challenging. It wasn't until I stood before the class on the last day of school that I realized that my two 8th graders wouldn't be there anymore. I nearly cried as I dismissed everyone, row by row, and I kept George and Rhonda back until the end. As we shook hands, I saw in their eyes and felt in my heart that we had been through a lot together, and it had been good. All of us had grown and learned a lot about each other from struggles, a few successes, and lots of trying.

In the five years since then, I've added grades K through 4 to my class and I've fallen into the groove of getting most everything in that I need to, but never quite all. There's always something we haven't gotten to at the end of the day. People always ask how we do all the things we do, and I always have to say that I really don't know. We've prepared for many Christmas and Mother's Day programs, cleaned the school hundreds of times, gone on nature walks, bandaged minor injuries, finished countless art projects, gone on field trips, read great books together...done so many things, and of course, we've held classes and learned from and about each other.

And every year, it is harder and more painful to watch the 8th grade leave on the last day. It feels to me like I imagine it feels to parents as they watch their children leave home. I miss my graduates and worry whether they've learned what they need to know, and I look forward to their visits and to any news of how they're doing. Whenever we do get together, there are endless enjoyable and funny things to remember, and the school really does feel a lot like home to me. My students and I share a history that ordinary students and teachers never have the time to develop, and I wouldn't trade my experiences here for anything. I hope to have many more years to learn from my students as I try my best to teach them, one busy day at a time.

Jon Huber, New Elm Springs School,
Hutchinson County, 1992-98

Suggestions for Further Research, Thought and Discussion

1. Examine the history of your county to learn more about the one-room schools that were once established there. Find their locations, and visit those schoolhouses that remain. Visit a one-room school that has been restored.

2. Visit a one-teacher school that is in operation today.

3. Write an especially vivid memory of an episode in your own educational experience that has made a difference in your life.

4. Consider the ways in which the one-room school experiences of the Native Americans and immigrants were similar? How were they different?

5. Consider the types of hands-on learning that were part of the one-room school experience. Could such activities enhance education today?

Bibliography

Erpestad, David and David Wood. *Building South Dakota*. Pierre: South Dakota State Historical Society, 1997.

Fuller, Wayne E. *One-Room Schools of the Middle West*. Lawrence: University Press of Kansas, 1994.

Hallstrom, Linda and Maricarrol Kueter. *South Dakota Country School Days*. Dallas: Taylor Publishing Co., 1987.

Henke, Warren A. and Everett C. Albers, eds. *The Legacy of North Dakota's Country Schools.* Bismarck: ND Humanities Council, 1998.

Morgan, Ruth, ed. *Memoirs of South Dakota Retired Teachers.* Stickney, SD: Argus Printers, 1976.

National Education Association. *One Teacher Schools Today.* Washington, DC: NEA, 1960.

Parker, Donald Dean, ed. *History of Our County and State: Clay County.* Brookings: South Dakota State College, 1959.

Rankin, Dorothy, ed. *Country School Legacy: Humanities on the Frontier.* Silt, Colorado: Country School Legacy, 1981.

Schatzmann, Iman Elsie. *The Country School.* Chicago: University of Chicago Press, 1942.

Shoemaker, Eva. *Prairie Schools.* Philip, SD: West River Museum Society, 1982.

South Dakota Department of Education and Cultural Affairs. "1997 Fall Enrollment by Attendance Center." http://www.state.sd.us/state/executive/deca/data/97attn.htm.

THE SOUTH DAKOTA HUMANITIES COUNCIL was created in 1972 by the National Endowment for the Humanities (NEH) to give financial support to public humanities programs in the state. The humanities are academic disciplines concerned with people, their values and the human experience. The humanities include philosophy, ethics, comparative religion, jurisprudence, history, literature, archaeology, languages, linguistics, the history, theory and criticism of the arts, and those aspects of the social sciences which have humanities content and employ humanities methods. SDHC is an independent, nonprofit corporation supported by a grant from NEH and also by grants and gifts from private foundations, corporations and individuals. The Council, in turn, grants these funds to nonprofit groups and organizations to support humanities activities. The Humanities Council also administers Council-conducted projects, such as the Speaker's Bureau, Resource Center, Reading Series and Teacher Institutes. Additional information about the Council is available at our web site: www.sdstate.edu/~whum/http/home.html. Our e-mail address is sdhc@ur.sdstate.edu. Or you may write us for additional information: South Dakota Humanities Council, Box 7050, University Station, Brookings, SD 57007-2099.

THE SOUTH DAKOTA HUMANITIES FOUNDATION was formed in 1987 by former members of the South Dakota Humanities Council and other concerned citizens to further the work of the council. The Foundation is a separate, nonprofit corporation dedicated to providing financial resources in order to ensure the future stability, independence and financial strength of the SDHC. Funds raised by the Foundation are invested in an endowment fund. The Foundation actively seeks gifts to the endowment from individuals, the business community, and philanthropic foundations. Each gift the Foundation receives, no matter the size, is important because it generates the continuation of challenging and compelling humanities programs in South Dakota. In 1996, the South Dakota Humanities Council and the South Dakota Humanities Foundation received a $100,000 Challenge Grant from NEH to be matched by $300,000 in non-federal funds to be raised by July 2000. If you would like to contribute to the endowment, please write: South Dakota Humanities Foundation, Box 7050, University Station, Brookings, SD 57007-2099.

To purchase additional copies of
One-Room Country School
contact

South Dakota Humanities Foundation
P.O. Box 7050 University Station
Brookings, SD 57007-2099

Quantity discounts are available. Write us at the above address or call
us at (605) 688-6113. Our fax number is (605) 688-4531.
You may also reach us by Email: SDSU_SDHC@sdstate.edu or

Visit our web site: http://web.sdstate.edu/humanities/